The Art and Science of Child Management

George R. Mount

Sharon R. Walters

Mountain View College

Dallas, Texas

**KENDALL/HUNT
PUBLISHING COMPANY**
Dubuque, Iowa

B   402606   01

Contents

Foreword **vii**
Preface **ix**
Introduction **xi**

Chapter 1. Pitfalls in a Child's World 1

The Skilled Caretaker **1**
Guidelines for Caretakers **4**

Chapter 2. Principles for Changing Behavior 7

Observation **7**
A Method for Accurate Observation **7**
Arranging Contingencies That Work **8**
Changing Behavior **9**
Changing Consequences: The Effects of Behavior Positive Reinforcement **10**
    Fig. 1 Identifying Potential Reinforcers With Children **13**
    Fig. 2 Graph of Minutes Spent Playing the Piano the First Three Weeks **13**
    Fig. 3 Graph of Minutes Spent Playing the Piano the Second Three Weeks **15**
    Fig. 4 Immediate vs Longterm Consequences and Examples **16**
Negative Reinforcement **16**
Punishment **17**
Punishment Used Correctly **18**
How to Use Punishment Correctly **18**
Inconsistent Punishment **19**
Natural Punishing Consequences **21**
Punishment Used Incorrectly **21**
Side Effects of Punishment **22**
Extinction **23**
    Fig. 5 Graph of Extinction of "Mommy May I" Behavior, Spontaneous Recovery and Re-extinction **24**

Chapter 3. Communicating Effectively 25

Ineffective Communication **25**
Guilt Inducing Communication **25**
Colored Hearing **26**
Effective Communication **27**
Talking It Over **27**
Recognizing His Feelings **27**
Alternatives **28**
Active Listening **28**
I vs. You Messages **29**
No-Lose Approach **29**
Family Communication **30**
Communicating about the Birds and the Bees **31**

Chapter 4. Early Social Learning and Development 33

Learning: A Definition **33**
Three Ways to Learn **33**
Operant Conditioning **34**
Modeling **35**
Classical Conditioning of Emotions **35**
Classical Conditioning: A Technical Explanation **36**
The Importance of Classical Conditioning **37**
Extinguishing Inappropriate Reactions **37**
Spontaneous Recovery **38**
Generalization of Conditioned Emotional Reactions **38**
Learned Helplessness: A Theory Which Relates to the Causes and Treatment Of Depression, Anxiety And Motivational Difficulties **39**
The Caretaker as a Teacher **41**

Chapter 5. Emotional Reactions 43

Signs of Stress and Anxiety **43**
Frustration and Emotion **44**
Fear **45**
Sources of Fear **46**
    Physical support **46**
    Financial security **46**
    Divorce **46**
    Fantasy **47**
    Guilt **48**
    Fear of Failure **49**

Fear, Failure and Performance **50**
Fig. 6 Graph of the Relationship Between Anxiety and Performance **51**
Fear of Failure and Loss of Self Esteem **51**
Competition and Jealousy **52**
Rejection **52**
Health fears **53**
Grief **54**

Chapter 6. Early Development of The Child 57

The Unborn Child **57**
The Fetus That Learns **57**
Cognitive Development **59**
Fig. 7 Examples of Child Development from Birth to 12 years **60**
The Development of Moral Thought **62**
Self Control and Delayed Gratification **62**
Social Development **63**
Sex-Role Development **64**
Sexual Awareness **65**

Chapter 7. Language, Intelligence, and Creativity 67

Communication **67**
Selective Reinforcement **67**
Imitation **68**
Questions **68**
Words: The Meaning and Power of Words **68**
Intelligence and Language **69**
Thinking: A Covert Language **70**
Rules **70**
Intelligence **71**
Creativity **72**
Learning to Be Creative **72**
Fact and Fantasy **73**
Becoming Creative **74**

Chapter 8. Adjustment Problems and Their Treatment 75

Spotting Problem Behaviors **75**
Characteristics: The Type A, B, and C Child **76**
Abnormal Behavior: A Definition **77**
How Abnormal Behavior Comes About **78**

Coping Skills **78**
The Depressed Child **79**
Signs of Suicide **79**
Problems That Aren't Problems **80**
How Do You Find Professional Counseling for the Child **82**
What Kinds of Treatment Might Be Expected **82**

Chapter 9. More Principles of Child Management 85

Shaping **85**
Schedules of Reinforcement **86**
Fixed Ratio Schedules **86**
Variable Ratio Schedules **87**
Interval Schedules of Reinforcement **87**
Fixed Interval Schedules **87**
Variable Interval Schedules **88**
Discrimination **88**
Generalization **89**

Chapter 10. Ideas for Behavior Programs 91

Eight Examples **91**
Fading Out Programs **96**

References **97**

Foreword

Whether through parenting or a profession, dealing with children on a daily basis is one of the most difficult tasks facing many adults. Lay advice and vague value statements help very little.

To effectively manage children, parents and professionals alike need both knowledge of normal development and techniques for intervening when the child's development needs guidance. These techniques need to come from a variety of theoretical approaches as well as from well grounded research and clinical experiences. Furthermore, these techniques must be specific and explained with examples.

The Art and Science of Child Management by Dr. Mount and Ms. Walters meets all these requirements, and, by doing so, it should be extremely helpful to all those who raise or work with children.

Randy Price, M.S.
Instructor of Child Development
Richland College
Dallas, Texas

Introduction

Have you ever wondered why children are the way they are? It is obvious that there are many differences among children. One child may be the class whiz kid who is always polite while his sibling is a holy terror who always does poorly. Do such differences occur by chance? Is one child just born to be dull and troublesome, while the other is born smart?

At one time, many people believed that a person's life was predestined to be good or bad. We now believe that the environment into which an individual is born plays a large part in determining how well one copes throughout his life. It is from this environment that the child learns right from wrong and which goals are desirable and which are not. This book takes the point of view that human behavior is predictable, mostly learned, and more importantly, that behavior can be changed. If we make the right changes, we will get any changes in behavior that we wish.

As caretakers*, we often attempt to change the child's behavior and, despite our good intentions, we do not always get the child to change in the way we thought he would. Our inability to see into the future makes decisions about the child's life extremely difficult. We want his early experiences to help him later in life, but it is difficult to see how experiences he has now will effect his adult life.

The following chapters provide basic guidelines for caretakers which are based on recent research and on the clinical experiences of two concerned professionals. We hope that this book will help minimize the many problems which parents face and insure the success of your child.

Our point of view is a positive one. Numerous problems dealing with children can be overcome with the procedures outlined in this book. This book takes the position that everyone's child has great potential which will be realized with sound guidance. In the past it was believed that a child must be born with talent to be great, yet research has not found this to be true. Beyond the physical build, it appears that the way the child is raised is the most important determinant. Aside from certain physical advantages, like height or size, the concept of "inborn talent" is mostly a myth. Any child can be a talented scientist, artist, and/or leader if he is raised in the proper environment. The child is much like a tree. Given an inconsistent and inadequate environment its potential will be stunted. Given a consistent and nourishing environment it will become strong and fruitful.

*The term caretaker is a general one used by many psychologists to refer to any person that cares for the child. Therefore, our use of the term includes parents, teachers, and other child care professionals.

Preface

The Art and Science of Child Management was written for a wide range of individuals. It was intended as a book for parents and child care professionals as well as a supplement for high school and college level courses. Therefore, certain technical information has been included that can be omitted without distorting the meaning or usefulness of the book. The textual material and examples provide the foundation for our approach while the material presented in boxes contain more technical explanations and examples for those interested in a more academic treatment of the subject.

This book is the result of many years of experience dealing with children and their caretakers. A few relevant references are provided for those caring to pursue special topics. It is, of course, impossible to reference every source that has helped shape our present position.

We would like to thank Randy Price, Dr. John Pope, Dr. Dan and Fredda Perkins, Tom Payton, and Pat Barnes for their suggestions and contributions to the manuscript. Also, we appreciate Wayne Hulon's illustrations and Dr. Mike Sink's efforts to improve our grammer. However, we take the responsibility for any shortcomings the book might possess.

Chapter 1

Pitfalls in a Child's World

The Skilled Caretaker

How good is your memory? Can you remember what it was like to be a child? Our childhood recollections are likely to be a mixture of pleasant and painful memories. As we think back over the pleasant times, we may find ourselves wishing that things could again be that simple or that exciting. As we consider the painful events in our past, we may even now feel uncomfortable or unfinished as we recall them. We find ourselves wishing that these events had never happened. We may even try to block these events from our mind in order to defend ourselves from the pain and anxiety which comes with this memory.

As caretakers, we often concern ourselves with making a better life for our children. We want to shield them from the pain we felt and improve their chances for success. These are noble goals, but the path to these goals is often unclear. The child's world of today is different from that which we knew as children. Along with all the new conveniences and advantages have come many new pitfalls for the child. Guiding the child around these pitfalls and motivating him toward self-actualization can be difficult. We find ourselves wondering how much "push" is too much and will he be spoiled if we let him do his own thing? And what about drugs and street violence?

The child's world of today is a complex one. We cannot control all of the negative influences that may be harmful to our child. In the course of his life, he will find himself in situations where dangerous or anti-social acts seem to be the "thing to do" at the moment. How will your child bear up under peer pressures? When the gang decides to try a new psychedelic drug or jump off the second floor balcony into the wading pool, will he be the first one in line, or will he be the kind of person who can say "I'd rather not" and still keep his friends? And then there is the increased competition for jobs which has led to pressure to succeed. Will he make the grade in school or drop out? Can he cope with job pressure or will he have ulcers by age 30?

Even though it is impossible to filter out all the negative influences, it is possible to guide the child around many pitfalls. As caretakers, our influence can be of great importance in determining the direction of the child's life. Some caretakers react to this idea with the objection that they do not want to tell the child; they want him to be an individual and make his own decisions about what is right or wrong. If these caretakers will look closer, they will see that they do control the direction of their children's lives. These individuals would not allow a child to step out into a busy street. They do not allow them to eat whatever they want. They teach them that it's good to get an education. What they do does influence the future of the child.

To be sure, some caretakers do not control the children in their care. They may let the child do whatever he chooses. They may have good intentions of letting the child "do his own thing," or sometimes they just don't want to put in the time that it takes to raise a child correctly. Often, parents want to do something about their child's behavior, but they don't know how. Whenever they try to teach or guide their child, he loudly complains that they are cruel and controlling. He stubbornly asserts that it's his life and he can live it his way.

Initially, the child is very immediate and impulsive. He wants everything now! He has very little control over his own behavior. Jim may not want to hurt sister Susie, but she has that tempting new toy and he can't wait, so he hits her to get it. He may receive a new toy for his birthday and promptly destroy it, because he just had to see what would happen when it fell from the roof. He may know that eating a whole bag of candy will make him sick, but it tastes good right then. He wants everything now! He wants his cake and he wants to eat it, too!

When the child is allowed to do whatever he wants, whenever he wants he appears to enjoy this freedom immensely. Later, he may regret the consequences of his impulsiveness. He may feel guilty for hitting Susie and the guilt can stay with him for a long time. He may be sorry that he no longer has his new toy. When he is feeling sick from eating that whole bag of candy he may hate himself for being so silly. This lack of control over his own behavior is the beginning of low self esteem and a poor self image. The child feels limited. He feels he can't do right, he can't succeed, and he can't be good. This feeling is too often reinforced by others who say "See I told you what would happen" or "You have been a bad child for doing those things."

The irony here is that this is the child who is allowed to do whatever he wants, whenever he wants; he always gets his way, yet he feels limited, and bad about himself. These spoiled children may seem to push their caretakers to their limits as though they were asking for punishment. Some of these children push parents to their limits because they feel that they deserve punishment. They know that their behavior alienates others and they want someone to help them stop. They want to be likeable, but all they hear is what a troublemaker they are, or how hardheaded they are. Such labels tend to be realized, they are self-fulfilling prophecies. The child learns that he is a hardheaded troublemaker and so he behaves accordingly. This child is likely to be tomorrow's juvenile delinquent.

Such antisocial behavior may be a way of getting their caretaker's attention. It is a way of finding out if their caretakers really care. Children appreciate reasonable limits. In one sense, the parent who goes to the trouble of watching what the child is doing and places restraints on the child's behavior is showing the child that he cares. He is paying attention to the child and taking the time to guide him around pitfalls which the child may be too inexperienced to see or too impulsive to avoid. The permissive parent, though often warm and loving, makes few demands for mature behavior. Such parents are likely to be lax in their use of praise and discipline. The children of such parents have been found to be immature, highly dependent, lacking in self-control, and tending to withdraw from novel or stressful situations. (Baumrind, 1967) Furthermore, the child of such parents is not likely to be achievement orientated or socially responsible. (Baumrind, 1971) Some parents go to the other extreme; they are highly controlling, using coercion rather than reason. They are intolerant of disagreement and are not very affectionate or sympathetic toward the child. The children of these authoritarian parents tend to be somewhat self-reliant and self-controlled, but they are also relatively discontented, insecure, distrustful, withdrawn, and uninterested in friendships. (Baumrind, 1967) So, excessive restraint also has its pitfalls. The child that has been excessively punished, overly restrained, and made to feel very guilty, goes through life doubting their worth, their decisions, and their ability. They are eternally self-critical and anxious of what others will think.

The child who is repeatedly warned about various pitfalls is likely to be seen as fearful and anxious. They may avoid many activities, preferring the safety of home. To be sure, they avoid many pitfalls, but their freedom is limited and unhappiness is too often a result. The child who is repeatedly cautioned can also rebel, exhibiting strong counter control. This child takes the course of a daredevil, delighting in scaring others with his reckless feats. He will not do what he is told even if it is what he was thinking of doing.

So who is to know how much restraint is enough? How can a parent know which behaviors to punish and which to praise? The art and science of rearing a child is neglected in our culture. Our schools teach many skills, but very few touch upon the most important occupation of all, that of caretaker. Caretaking is both an art and a science. It is a highly technical, full time occupation.

As caretakers we would like to have children that are mature, content, competent, self-reliant, self-controlled, realistic, curious, and good at making friends. Baumrind (1967) found that such children are likely to have parents who are warm, loving, and good at communicating with their children. Unlike permissive parents, these parents exerted considerable control and demanded mature behavior from their children. While they were firm in their opinions and clear about the reasons for their directions, they respected the independence and decisions of their children. This combination of control and support for independence was called authoritative parental behavior. (Baumrind, 1967)

Guidelines for Caretakers

The authors would like to offer the following guidelines for caretakers.

1. Be consistent—Decide what behavior will be rewarded and which will be punished. Inconsistent discipline is confusing to the child. Don't change what's right or wrong whenever following through becomes a little inconvenient. Approval or disapproval should not depend on the caretaker's mood.
2. Be flexible—Admit when you are wrong. You do not have to appear perfect. The child will eventually see through a false image of perfection and become disenchanted. If they do model your perfectionism, they may adopt unrealistically high standards for themselves and others.
3. Be open to change—If the situation changes, rules can change. As the child becomes older and proves himself more responsible, fewer rules will be necessary.
4. Be honest—When the child is being obnoxious you don't have to love that behavior even though you love the child. Example: "I like to have you with me when I shop, but I don't like to hear you whine for things you want. I feel like leaving you home when you whine."
5. Be specific—Tell the child exactly what you want and don't want him to do. Tell him exactly what will happen if he continues to misbehave. Example: Don't say, "Stop acting like an ape or I'll string you up like a bunch of bananas." Say, "I'd like you to stop swinging from the grocery cart or you will have to wait in the front of the store." Remember, caretakers that use idle threats have deaf children.
6. Suggest constructive alternatives—Example: "If you want to swing, you can do that when we get home. Right now, I'd like you to decide what you would like me to buy for dessert tonight."
7. Talk in a quiet and respectful voice—There is no reason to use an angry or sarcastic tone. After a calm reminder, wait a minute to see if he will comply and then reward or punish as indicated.
8. Punish specific acts, not character—Remind the child that it is his behavior that you do not like, not his character. Praise specific behaviors rather than global positives like, "You're always such a wonderful, creative, obedient, etc., child." Specific comments such as, "I really enjoyed hearing you play that new song on the piano" are best.

9. Use imitation—Children are great imitators. When a child is first learning a new behavior show them how. Also, remember that children see what you do and may copy your actions. Example: Bobby's dad tells him that it's dangerous to ride a bike without holding on to both handles. Later, Bobby sees his dad holding a sandwich while riding a bike.

10. Teach independence—Gradually withdraw your help and attention as the child masters new behavior. Give praise intermittently thereafter in order to maintain the behavior.

11. Avoid power struggles whenever possible—Use ingenuity and reasoning to work around difficulties without arguing. The child has a right to his beliefs and misbehaviors. They should, however, be willing to accept the consequences of their behaviors.

12. Give small children plenty of time to follow instructions—Children become confused and resentful when hurried. Let the child know the day's schedule so he can adjust his plans.

13. Children need to learn self-reliance as well as cooperation—Step into arguments between children *only* to prevent physical injury or to teach a socially appropriate solution. When fights are prolonged, separate the children for a short period telling them they won't be allowed to play with each other if they can't learn to solve their differences.

14. Encourage curiosity—Children's questioning and exploring natures are the cornerstone of later intellectual and creative achievement.

15. Be affectionate—Touching, hugging, and kissing should be part of the child's daily life. Older children and adolescents also need affection from *both* parents.

Chapter 2

Principles for Changing Behavior

Studies in behavior have found that behavior is relatively orderly and predictable. In general, it may be said that human beings seek out and engage in those activities which lessen stress and provide rewards. They move away from situations and do not tend to repeat acts which have undesirable results. From these basic principles, we could predict what a child will do at a given time if we knew in advance what things he thinks are rewarding, stressful, or undesirable. If all children were raised alike, predicting their behavior would be easy. We would, however, have a very dull world, because everyone would behave in much the same way. Since identical child rearing is far from the case, the most effective way to predict behavior is to observe what the child has done in the past, in similar circumstances.

Observation

The key to prediction is observation. For example: Each time we serve spinach to Junior, we may observe that he leaves it on the plate and that his mother's nagging does not convince him to eat it. We may *observe* that he always asks for two helpings of tutti-frutti ice cream. We may *predict* that he will do the same the next time these foods are served.

During observation, many aspects of the situation are important. Observation of the situation, the frequency of that behavior, and the caretaker's reaction to the behavior can give important clues as to the best way to change the probability a particular behavior will occur. For example: If we tell Junior that he must eat the spinach, which is good for him, before he gets his tutti-frutti ice cream, then we may *change* his habit of leaving the spinach.

A Method for Accurate Observation

The better our observations, the more accurately we can predict and make changes in behavior patterns. Accurate observation can be difficult. In our everyday rush there may not always be time or opportunity to observe as well as one would wish. Also, even very subtle aspects of behavior, like a mother's sarcastic tone can profoundly influence the behavioral pattern being observed. The following method has been used successfully for many years by teachers, parents, and professionals to increase their powers of observation. According to this method, human behavior can be seen as involving three observable components: (1) A *stimulus* which can be any aspect in our environment that we can perceive. (i.e. birds, music, trees, rain, hunger pains, words, thoughts) (2) A *response* (or behavior) is anything people do, that is behavior in general. (i.e. talking, writing, singing, thinking, dancing) (3) A *consequence* (outcome) is anything that happens to the individual as a result of their behavior (i.e. falling off a log, winning a game, feeling good).*

i.e. Stimulus ⟶   Response ⟶   Consequence

(1) (a) *Stimulus* ⟶   *Response* ⟶   *Consequence*
      Up coming math test   Bobby studies hard   Bobby receives an A

     (b) *Stimulus* ⟶   *Response* ⟶   *Consequence*
     Linda sees Sue's new   Linda steals toy   Linda's mother
     toy   makes her give back
                                                the toy and go to her
                                                room

     (c) *Stimulus* ⟶   *Response* ⟶   *Consequence*
     Child sees box   Child opens box   Nothing is inside of it

Arranging Contingencies That Work

The above sequence of Stimulus → Response → Consequence is called a contangency. A contingency is a relation between events. If one event occurs, then another event will follow. In any given situation, the occurrence of some predetermined consequence for a particular response is contingent upon the child's emitting a particular response. Wesley Becker, in his book *Parents Are Teachers,* advocates giving direction to children in the form of a contingency, that is, a rule will specify the behavior required and then its consequence. Furthermore, he suggests stating rules in a short and positive way so that they will be easy to remember.

---

*Note: A consequence is also a stimulus because it is an event that is perceptable.

Examples:

Correct	Incorrect
Homework before playing outside.	You better do your homework or you'll be sorry.
You straighten your room before you leave for the game.	Wait till your father sees your room.
If you get ready for school by 7:30 you get to watch cartoons.	If you are not ready for school you will miss your bus.

Once the rule (or contingency) has been delivered, whether or not the child complies depends on the type of consequence. Thus, behavior is controlled by its consequences (Skinner, 1953) and providing specific rules is an important part of child management. We can view all behavior as a continuous flow of stimuli (events), responses (behavior), and consequences. We are constantly interacting with our environment; for example, we can view example (b) above in terms of its affect upon Sue instead of Linda. Linda steals Sue's toy (stimulus), Sue crys (response), Linda's mother returns the toy (consequence). The outcome of a response generally has some consequence for the individual. This consequence may be seen by him as being desirable (reinforcing), aversive (punishing), or neutral (extinction).

As stated before, we may predict that human beings will seek out and engage in those activities which minimize stress and provide rewards. They move away from situations and do not tend to repeat acts which result in undesirable consequences.

If we become good observers of behavior we will be able to predict and even change the probability that a sequence of behavioral events will again occur. In the examples above, we might predict that Bobby will continue to study hard if the grade of A is a desirable consequence; and that Linda will be less likely to steal Sue's toys if having to stay in her room is aversive. Likewise, the small child may not bother to open the box again because nothing of interest was inside.

Changing Behavior

Once you have observed the behavior you wish to change, decide exactly what new changes you want. There are two ways to change a behavioral response. One is by changing the consequences for the behavioral response so that the child alters his behavior. Another way is by changing the stimulus event which sets the occasion for the undesired response to occur.

Changing the stimulus event that cues the undesirable behavior can often be done more easily than changing the consequences for that response, as illustrated by these examples. (1) Toddling Todd is not yet able to control his curiosity, so mother puts all the breakable and dangerous objects up on high shelves. So now the house is "toddler proof" and mother doesn't have to worry or scold. (2) The children always get into grandma's candy dish and ruin their dinner, so mother calls ahead and asks grandma to put the candy away and not offer it until after dinner. (3) Ms. Fitch discovers that Billy always rejects her commands when she uses an authoritative tone, so she learns to speak with a respectful tone.

Changing Consequences: The Effects of Behavior
Positive Reinforcement

Consequences which the person will work to obtain are called *positive reinforcers*. The term positive reinforcer may be defined as any stimulus (or event) which increases the probability that the response which it follows will occur again in a similar situation. You may think that this definition sounds like a fancy way to describe what happens when we reward someone. The term "reward" however, does not imply that the probability of the response which brought about the reward will increase. For example: Bob goes to the fair. Bob wants to try for a prize by throwing baseballs (stimulus event). Bob tries (response) and is rewarded (consequence) with a rosy cheeked baby doll. On subsequent occasions at the fair, Bob does not stop to throw baseballs. In this example, the baby doll was a reward, but it was not a positive reinforcer because Bob never played that game again. Here is another example: Eight year old Andy felt no one paid him much attention. Whenever he felt lonely (stimulus event), he would pull the fire alarm at school (response) and then he would get into trouble and receive much attention (consequence). Andy did this often. Most of us certainly wouldn't call getting into trouble a reward

or desirable event, but for a very lonely boy, attention (either positive or negative) can be very positively reinforcing. The term "reinforcer" was developed, then, because the term "reward" doesn't apply in quite the same way.

As parents, you can use the principle of reinforcement to increase positive behaviors in your child and decrease the time he spends doing things that aren't functional. Ideally, the use of natural consequences is the best. If possible, use praise and attention.

If occasional praise is not enough, the creative caretakers can often arrange situations that will positively reinforce good behaviors with natural consequences. For example: (1) Tell relatives and friends about the child's latest accomplishments so they can praise him. (2) Athletic instructors can organize a mini competition or show at the end of each week so the children can cheer for each other. (3) Parents can ask children to briefly entertain for visitors. (4) Parents can take new visitors for a tour of the house being sure to comment on how nicely decorated and cleanly kept their child's room is. If the child isn't listening, the parents can be sure and relay any compliments visitors made about his or her room.

The use of objects like money as reinforcers is *only* recommended when the natural reinforcers are not working or when the behavior would normally be reinforced by material reinforcers in the environment.

Behaviors to be positively reinforced with objects	*Behaviors expected without material reinforcers*
selling handicraft items made by the child	cleaning his room
	caring for his pet
doing unassigned chores	putting away his bike
mowing the neighbor's yard	remembering lunch money

The following is a list of consequences which are often effective in changing childrens behaviors: *Social reinforcers*—praise, attention, recognition, playing a game, compliments, strokes (touching), acceptance, running errands, eye contact, smiles, playing Jacks, listening to music. *Object reinforcers*—snacks, TV time, movies, amusement park tickets, eating out, money, prizes, clothes. *Things which usually work as punishers*—criticisms, reminders, spankings, loss of money, loss of privileges, loss of TV time, staying in room or house.

To use the principle of positive reinforcement, you must first be an accurate observer. The following steps will illustrate how you could use behavioral principles to increase the amount of time a child spends practicing the piano.

Step 1: *Specify* a goal behavior. Decide exactly what behavior you desire to see changed and what responses the child will emit when the program succeeds.

Step 2: *Observe* what activities are reinforcers for the child. These will be the things he prefers to spend his time doing and the places he asks to go. Figure 1 contains a more detailed procedure for determining positive reinforcers.

Step 3: *Record* how many minutes the child plays the piano over the period of a week or two. We will call this period of time a *baseline* observation (see Figure 2).

Step 4: *Decide* what you think might be a good reinforcer for this behavior, and then make obtaining this reinforcer contingent on the child's completion of a specified number of hours of practice. Be sure and tell the child exactly what he will get and how much he must practice.

Step 5: Continuously *observe* and *record* the number of hours practiced.

Step 6: *Follow through and be consistent.* Positively reinforce him if he completes the full five hours, but not if he only practices four hours and 45 minutes. If you reinforce him in the latter case, next week he may only practice four hours and 35 minutes and then only four hours, etc.

Step 7: *Re-evaluate* your procedure often. If the child is failing to meet the criteria, several things may be wrong. What you are asking may be too difficult or, more likely, the reinforcer is not really desirable.

Reinforcers with Children

A. Ask the following questions:

1. If you were going into a store to buy some toys what would you get?
2. What are three jobs you like best to do at home?
3. If you could do anything or go somewhere with one (or both) of your parents, what would you like best?

B. Things to do:

1. Note what activities the child prefers to spend his time doing and note which ones he asks to do most often.

   (High probability activities can be used as reinforcers for low probability responses. This is like the work first, play later philosophy.)
2. Go with the child to the dime store and note which toys he is attracted to.
3. Things like getting to leave school at lunch to go to the Dairy Queen, having friends over on weekends, going outside to play, and TV time are often powerful.
4. Become more aware of the positive effects of your praise and attention.

Figure 1. Identifying potential reinforcers with children.

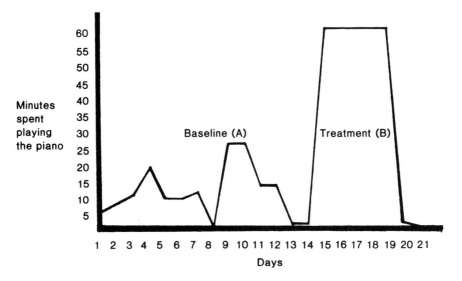

Figure 2. Graph of minutes spent playing the piano the first three weeks.

Let's take the case of Mozart, Jr., to illustrate how these steps work and how such programs can be changed when necessary.

Step 1: Mozart's mother wants him to learn to play more piano pieces.

Step 2: Mozart's mother observed that he frequently asks to go to the movies.

Step 3: She planned to increase his piano practicing time; and so, she took a two week baseline measure and recorded the number of hours practiced (see Figure 2). This turned out to be one hour per week.

Step 4: She told Mozart, Jr. that he could go to the movie on Sunday, if he practiced five hours that week.

Step 5: This worked fine for one week and . . .

Step 6: His mother took him to the show on Sunday. The following week, Mozart Jr. did not reach the five hours required and so stayed home.

Step 7: His mother decided that the reinforcement was insufficient and told him that he would also receive 2 dollars to take with him to the movie. After repeating Steps 1 through 6 again, Mozart's mother now reports that he practices 5 hours each week. She has, however, observed that Mozart Jr. always waits until the last minute to practice and so they end up at the Sunday midnight showing of "The Horror of the Jelly Monster."

Ideally, she would like him to practice one hour a day; but he always seems to have something else to do like hunt frogs, eat snacks, or watch Super Canary on T.V.

Such activities can be said to be *immediately reinforcing,* i.e. their consequences are immediate. They make us laugh or satisfy some immediate need. Going to the movies is fun, but for Mozart Jr., the end of the week is a long way away. Becoming a concert pianist sounds good, also, but that's years away. We can call these events, which are removed in time from the initial response, *long-term reinforcing consequences.*

Research has shown that short-term consequences are much more powerful than long-term ones. We tend to do those things which have immediate consequences and put off doing things which have delayed consequences. So, how are we going to get Mozart Jr. to be a concert pianist if he keeps chasing frogs instead of practicing?

Oftentimes, behavior programs are more successful if we make the consequences (reinforcer) more immediate. Instead of waiting until the end of the week to give Jr. his two dollars, we might decide that he should get 50¢ following an hour of practice on any day and, if he practices an hour a day for five days, he will get to go to a movie on the weekend. (see Figure 3)

Now, Mozart's mother reports that he diligently practices one hour a day, but she says that she is tired of hearing "Moon River" over and over and over. What we have now is quantity instead of quality. A better procedure would be to offer 50¢ extra for each piece of music that his teacher says he has correctly memorized. Mozart's mother should have been more specific about the goal behavior in Step One. Upon re-evaluation, (step 7) Mozart's mother now reports he is doing beautifully. Mozart's mother has kept a careful chart of his behavior:

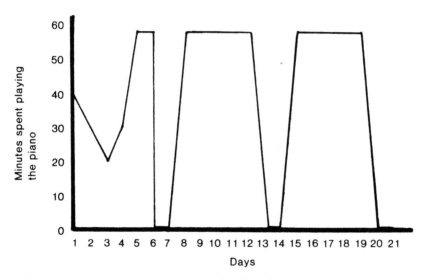

Figure 3. Graph of minutes spent playing the piano the second three weeks.

I. Immediate vs. Longterm Consequences

An *immediate consequence* is usually more powerful than a longterm consequence. This is especially true when a child is first learning. *Immediate reinforcement* means that the consequence of a certain behavior follows right after that behavior and increases its rate. Longterm reinforcement is delayed but it also increases the rate of a behavior. *Immediate punishment* is also more powerful. It decreases the rate of a behavior more rapidly than does longterm punishment.

II. Examples of Immediate Consequences vs. Longterm Consequences

eating snacks	gaining weight
smoking a cigarette	poor health
sleeping in class	flunking a test
eating candy	getting tooth decay
a peer's praise for misbehavior	a mother's disapproval when she finds out

Figure 4. Immediate vs. longterm consequences and examples.

Caution: Be careful not to set up a program so that lying or inconsistent behavior is reinforced. For example: Mom goes over to the neighbors' house for an hour. When she returns, Mozart Jr. says, "I practiced my hour." If Mom reinforces him for saying that he did, she may reinforce lying behavior. If she doesn't and he did practice, she may convey the idea that she doesn't trust him. It is best, then, to specify at the beginning that he will only receive credit when she is there to record the time or at a certain time of the day when she will always be home.

Negative Reinforcement

The concept of negative reinforcement is often confused with punishment. *Reinforcement,* by definition, always implies that some behavior increases. With punishment, one is attempting to suppress or stop some behavior from happening. A *negative reinforcer* can be defined as any stimulus or event which the individual will work to avoid. The following situations illustrate how negative reinforcement occurs in our lives every day.

Case 1 You turn on the shower and the water gets too hot (aversive stimulus) so you quickly learn to adjust the temperature (response).

Case 2 A small baby cries loudly (aversive stimulus). To the mother, this is a disturbing sound, so she runs to see what is wrong (response). The baby stops crying (consequence).

Case 3 The teacher's menacing stare (aversive stimulus) causes the children to stop talking and begin doing their school work (consequence).

In the above examples, cases 1 and 3 involve someone's doing something in order to *avoid* some consequences, while case 2 involves escape from some consequence. We can say that the escape or avoidance response is what is reinforced, i.e., changing water temperature, quieting baby, or doing school work quietly. In some cases, negative reinforcement may have undesirable results. The individual who is having a difficult time avoiding failing grades in school may escape this situation altogether by dropping out. Likewise, the woman who can't cope with the responsibilities of motherhood might turn to alcohol as a method of escape. The following example is derived from the principle of negative reinforcement.

> While Mom is driving the kids to the ball game, they become noisy and begin fighting with each other. She pulls off the road, stops the car, and begins to read a book. She calmly informs them that when they quiet down she will proceed to the game.

Negative reinforcement then, is similar to punishment in that aversive consequences are used; however, with negative reinforcement we are trying to get a behavior to happen, rather than stop it, as with punishment.

Punishment

A punisher may be defined as any stimulus or event which decreases the probability that a response will occur again in a similar situation. For example: Pig Pen's mother discovers a five day old banana peel in his room (stimulus event). Pig Pen will have to clean his room (response) or his mother has threatened to throw out his dirt garden (consequence).

This definition is very broad. By defining punishment in this way, some things which we usually assume to be punishers really aren't, and other things which we hadn't thought to be punishing actually are. The following examples will illustrate how this can happen:

> Robby is responsible for a barrage of spit wads which occurs each day in class. His teacher has scolded him over and over again, telling him "that's not nice." (Punisher?) Robby doesn't quit.

> Pig Pen's mother tells him that he can't watch Super Canary on T.V. if he forgets to clean the mud off his shoes (contingency). Pig Pen forgets again (response). He doesn't get to watch T.V. (punishing consequence?) Pig Pen still can't remember to clean his shoes (response on future occasions).

In the above examples, the consequence for misbehaving had no effect on the behavior in question, i.e., they were not punishers at all. It could be that Robby wants his teachers attention or that he likes making her mad. Likewise, it could be that Pig Pen doesn't care anything about Super Canary.

Punishment Used Correctly

It is best to let the child know what behaviors will be punished and with what consequences before he gets into trouble. In this way, the parent's role is one of providing guidance. Children are not born good or bad, nor do they automatically know right from wrong. They must learn which is the right way and which is the wrong way to behave.

How to Use Punishment Correctly

Punishment can be an effective suppressor of behaving if it is administered properly. Azrin and Holz (1966) have outlined the "laws" of punishment and we have provided the following guidelines based on their findings. If you cannot effectively use punishment try using positive reinforcement or some other technique because you are not likely to be successful unless you can use punishment appropriately.

1. Punish specific behaviors not vague general notions. For example; "Son, I told you not to play with that antique vase, now it is broken"; *not,* "You're always breaking things and you're going to catch it this time."
2. Do not attempt to punish if you cannot prevent avoidance of the punisher. If the child is able to circumvent the punisher successfully it will be ineffective.
3. Low levels of punishment tend to be ineffective. Never start with a mild punishment and gradually increase the level of aversiveness. Make the intensity and frequency as high as necessary throughout the punishment program.
4. Never pair punishment with positive reinforcement. However, it is wise to point out alternative behaviors that will result in positive reinforcement instead of punishment.
5. Alternatives to physical punishment include response cost and time-out, and these are likely to have fewer side effects. *Response cost* means that it is possible to engage in the behavior if you are willing to pay the price. Tickets for speeding and extra assignments for being late are examples. *Time-out* is actually time-out from reinforcement. The child is not allowed to engage in reinforcing behavior for a period of time. When the teacher puts the child in the hall for 15 minutes for not behaving, she is attempting to use time-out. To be effective, however, the environment from which the child is being removed must have been reinforcing and the environment in which the child is being placed must be either nonreinforcing or aversive.

To administer punishment there is no need to become emotional. A quiet, firm voice will do. Be sure to discuss with the child what he did, exactly how he can do better, and what the consequences are. Don't back down if he argues, lest you reinforce this inappropriate form of negotiation. Also, try to administer the consequence after the misdeed as soon as possible. For example: Bouncing Billy loves to do flips off the dresser on to the bed. Whenever his mom can catch him, she always says, "Wait until your father gets home." This delayed threat leaves much time for Bouncing Billy to get in extra flips since he is going to get in trouble anyway later. It also leaves time for Mom to forget. This practice puts his father in the villain's role and is unfair, as well as ineffective. A better solution would involve immediate consequences and the provision of an acceptable, alternative way of behaving. Perhaps Bouncing Billy's mother should enroll him in a YMCA trampoline class.

Inconsistent Punishment

When rules are not established and punishment is inconsistently applied, the child can become confused and anxious. He may behave erratically or become rigid in manner. If he is punished and positively reinforced for the same behavior, a sort of learned helplessness may result. The following example will show how a child can learn to be helpless and dependent:

Magnolia's parents were inconsistently critical of her behavior. Sometimes when she tried to do things for herself, they praised her but most of the time they found fault with her attempts to be independent. It seemed to her that she just couldn't do anything right; so, she just decided she was dumb and depended on others to do things for her. At age 55, her mother still drives her around in the car and her father still directs her life. She's never been married or had a job.

Magnolia's history can be contrasted with that of Mrs. Industrious whose parents were always encouraging and tolerant of well meant attempts at independence. Mrs. Industrious is now 60 and has had a stroke. She has reduced ability to use the muscles of her right side, but she always has a smile on the left side of her face and a twinkle in her eye.

Both of these ladies attended a community craft class. Mrs. Industrious couldn't talk much but she watched intently. Soon she was making all kinds of nice things. Many of the other ladies, including Magnolia, spent a lot of time talking about how "untalented" they were and waiting for the instructor to show them how, just one more time.

Magnolia had her mother drive her to the center on other days for extra help. Toward the end of each session, she would repeatedly check to see if Mother had come so that she would not make her mother wait.

With much positive reinforcement and patience on the part of the instructor, Magnolia did much better. For the first time in her life, she actually had some nice pieces which she could say she had made. She began to show more independence and even walked to the center when her mother was not able to bring her. On one occasion, her mother arrived early and instead of rushing out, she firmly stated, "She can just wait until I am finished." The instructor wondered if adolescence could begin at age 55.

When criticism and failure might be the resulting consequences, the learned helplessness child avoids competing with others. It also allows him to avoid doing tasks which are dull or hard. If he is told to bring the clean clothes in off the line and drops them, mother probably will be critical and won't ask such a clumsy child to do such chores.

The sad thing is that after a while the child will begin to do less and less for himself. He may miss out, as Magnolia had, on many of the good things in life which require effort to achieve.

As you can see from the above discussion, punishment procedures have their problems and should be avoided if possible. Positive reinforcement is the best way to influence children's behavior. When stronger measures are required, negative reinforcement should be tried first. The rule is: use the least aversive consequence necessary to achieve the desired behavior. Only in extreme cases in which the child is endangering himself or others should strong measures like corporal* punishment be used. The following is such a case:

Benny had been in and out of hospitals since age three. At age nine, he was finally brought to a behavioral center. His eyes were both black and his head was bleeding. Ten minutes of observation revealed that these injuries were due to his head banging behavior. This child would utter a loud scream for no apparent reason and then bang his head against a wall or with his fist (response). His mother would sometimes hold him to make him stop or slap his hands (consequence). Nothing, however, appeared to work with Benny. Several doctors had recommended that he be institutionalized where he could be kept in a strait jacket and padded cell. At the behavior center, a procedure using small amounts of electrical shock was tried. This procedure took about eight hours over a two day period to reduce Benny's head banging to a low and nondangerous level. Benny has now learned to talk and even read a little. The point here is that several days of discomfort saved a child from an institutionalized life.

You may find that when you first try to apply some of the procedures that this book suggests, your child may groan and moan; however, if you are correctly applying these principles he will soon accept them. The time and effort you spend now may save you many tears and much trouble at a later time.

*Physical punishment, spanking, paddling, and/or the use of force.

Natural Punishing Consequences

Rudolf Dreikurs, author of *Children: The Challenge,* believes that using natural consequences is more effective than devised punishment procedures. He feels that punishment is used too often in a way that is meant to dominate the child, and this doesn't work well in our modern day democratic society. Punishment often only serves to strengthen children's resistance and increase their efforts to assert their rights. We need to use respectful methods which give the child credit for being able to control himself and make good decisions.

Many times the consequence that would ordinarily follow the child's misbehavior will be aversive enough to dissuade him or cause him to correct his own behavior. To discover what the natural consequence of a behavior is just ask yourself what would be the result of that response if you were not there to coach the child and, also, what would happen if the child acted this way around others. If the natural consequence is one that is fitting, then let nature take its course and don't interfere.

Examples of Natural Consequences:

1. Billy forgets his lunch money and he goes hungry for the day.
2. Susie didn't put her favorite dress in the hamper so it didn't get washed.
3. Dimples wanders away from her mother at the store. Instead of frantically looking for her, mother continues to shop. Dimples has to look to find her mother instead of getting the attention she *wanted* for her misbehavior.
4. Eddy leaves his new bike unlocked and it gets stolen. His parents tell him they're sorry and suggest he save his money for another.

While many parents may be anxious about letting their child go hungry or wear dirty clothes, this method teaches responsibility. Children whose caretakers constantly remind have the most forgetful children of all. They have no need to *learn* or *remember.* Parents who buy replacements for carelessly ruined items have destructive children. Parents who constantly correct children spend a lot of time engaged in power struggles, thus giving the child the attention his misbehavior was designed to get. (Dreikurs, 1964)

Punishment Used Incorrectly

The following are examples of how we can inadvertently punish desired behaviors. Percy sees some other boys writing dirty words on the walls at school (stimulus event). He tells his mother (response). His mother becomes very angry and gives him a five minute lecture about such things (punishing consequence). Percy decides he won't tell his mother about things that happen at school (subsequent response). It's Mother's birthday (stimulus event) and Mary decides to bring her breakfast, but she spills coffee in the bed (response).

Mother becomes very angry (punishing consequence). On subsequent occasions, Mary is very reluctant about trying to do nice things for her mother. Polly Anna and Miss Fudd are talking about their lesson plans (stimulus event). Polly Anna says, "I really would like to try this new program for slow learners" (response). Miss Fudd says, "Oh, why bother. Those new methods never work." (punishing consequence) Polly Anna becomes discouraged and doesn't try the program.

Side Effects of Punishment

Punishment has the advantage of having an immediate effect on the behavior we want to stop. The child who is picking his mother's daffodils will usually stop immediately when swatted on the rear. Punishment has side effects, however, which can make its use undesirable (Azrin & Holz, 1966). One of those side effects is that aversive consequences usually result in emotional responses and negative feelings toward the one who administers the punishment. The parent then may become associated with punishment and the child may begin to avoid the parent. Additionally, it is easy for the child to see when the parent is there to punish him and when the parent will not be aware of his behavior. We can say that the child "discriminates" the presence or absence of punishment. An example of this discrimination occurs when a class of children acts very good for one teacher and are reported to be unmanageable by another. A look at the difference in each teacher's discipline methods may be quite revealing. Let's look at some of the differences between Mrs. Constance's and Mrs. Lax's methods of discipline:

Mrs. Constance has set rules to go by and has made her class aware of these rules. They know when they can play and when they are supposed to work. When they come up to her desk without permission, they have learned that they will not receive attention. They have also learned that when they finish their work quickly and correctly, they receive free time and special surprises. When anyone misbehaves, he loses his free time privileges.

Mrs. Lax's rules are not so clear. When she has a headache, there are a lot of rules but when she has had a nerve pill, then there aren't too many rules. Since her rules aren't fixed, the children do pretty much what they want. They are constantly coming to her desk and wandering around the room. She finds the only way to get them to work a little is to shout things like, "I'm going to skin you alive."

The first teacher uses positive and negative reinforcement to conduct her classroom. The key to her success is her consistent use of consequences and an accurate ability to observe. The second teacher certainly lacks these characteristics. Her shouting and use of empty threats are techniques which usually fail because they are not followed by real consequences.

Extinction

Extinction is an event which involves the withdrawal of reinforcement. Such withdrawal usually results in a gradual decrease in the occurrence of a response. For example: Ellen has always been able to get a certain brand of tea at a grocery store across town (stimulus event) but, the last four times she has gone (response) they have not had that tea (no reinforcement). She resolves not to go again (extinction).

In another example of extinction, a child who has always gotten attention (positive reinforcement) for hiding in the house, now learns that no one will come looking for him so he stops hiding (extinction).

Extinction can be used to correct the "Mommy May I" syndrome that most children have. When your child asks for something, find out why he wants it. Decide if what he wants is inappropriate. If so, simply tell the child "no" and why not once. Then play deaf to the repetition of "Mommy May I" (extinction). The child's begging may increase slightly at first, but it will soon begin to decrease. When you give in to the child after he has asked many times you reinforce his asking many, many times for something. This is called partial (or intermittent) reinforcement, not extinction. This schedule of reinforcement produces a very high rate of responding. He responds repetitively like the gamblers in Las Vegas who keep putting their money in the slot machines because every once in a while it pays off. Chapter nine explains the characteristics of several different schedules of reinforcement.

If we were to take data on a child with the "Mommy May I" syndrome we could count the number of times the child asked for something after we have said no. Figure 5 shows how these data would look if plotted each day. After extinction is begun, you can see that the response rate will decrease so that you no longer have to listen to the child beg.

Sometimes a phenomena called *spontaneous recovery* will occur. For some unknown reason a previously extinguished response will occur again for a brief time. Spontaneous recovery most often occurs when the child has not been around you or in a particular situation for awhile. So he may come home from camp and spontaneously start to beg. If you continue to use extinction with his begging, he will quickly extinguish.

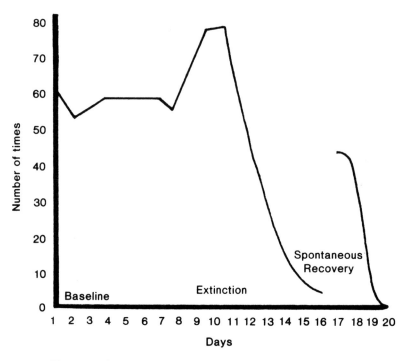

Figure 5. Graph of extinction of "Mommy may I" behavior, spontaneous recovery and re-extinction.

Chapter 3

Communicating Effectively

Ineffective Communication

Guilt Inducing Communication

Stern, moral lectures are used by many caretakers to control children's misbehavior. The problem with such lectures is that they don't just convey information about what is right or wrong, they also produce guilt feelings within the child. As a result, the child may develop behavioral problems as he attempts to relieve these feelings of guilt. The extent to which this type of communication causes problems will depend on several factors. If the child often receives stern criticism of his behavior, he may conclude that he is an unusually wicked brat who can do no better. When the person giving the lecture is someone the child looks up to, then the lecture is likely to have considerable guilt inducing impact. Lectures which leave the child feeling that what he has done is really unforgivable may lead him to develop some dysfunctional way to compensate for what he has done. He may become overly compliant and very dependent on others for direction. And, because others often differ in their ideas of what is wrong, he will often be confused and indecisive. Such a child is easily led and may, in later life, join a cult group which provides strict and perhaps bizarre guidance. Sometimes unusual compulsive behaviors like handwashing develop as a way of fending off the anxiety that guilt producing lectures engender.

Another way the child can deal with guilt feelings is to find a way to reject the caretaker or the content of the lecture. So, children sometimes react with "I hate you," or worse. They begin to avoid the caretaker. Other times, they may deny what they have done and really convince themselves that "it wasn't me." The child who frequently uses denial to relieve guilt feelings will be seen later, as the adult who never owns up to anything; it's always someone else's fault. Some children may just reject their parent's values so that they can be free of the guilt feelings which occur when they do not live up to their parents expectations. Such is often the case in very strict families who produce one or more juvenile delinquents. In other cases, rejecting an overly strict code of values or a dysfunctional family value system may be their only chance to live a normal life. Of course all children will occasionally show some tendency to blame others, deny their irresponsibility or depend on others for guidance.

It is only when these patterns are such that they will lead to social, academic, or legal problems that the caretaker should take action to help the child deal in a more constructive way with guilt feelings.

Colored Hearing

Sometimes what we hear is colored by our feelings:

Todd: "Mother, I would really rather you not come to school to hear me practice my violin. It distracts me and no one else's mother comes."

Mother: "You are embarrassed that I'm your mother? You are shutting me out of your life! I bought you that violin, didn't I?"

Todd: "All I asked was that you not come. I wish you would quit badgering me."

This mother did not clearly hear what her son was saying. What she heard was colored by a basic fear that she is somehow inferior and unloveable. Her reaction to her son's request is an attempt to make him feel guilty. It is designed to manipulate him into allowing her to continue attending practice sessions. It is designed to force him into saying that she does not embarrass him that he is proud of her. It is a passive way of getting back at him. This type of passive aggressive manipulation is indirect and often self-defeating. Even if Todd gives in to his mother's wishes, she is not likely to feel any better about herself because she had to manipulate him into saying what she wanted to hear.

Another side effect of passive aggressive actions is the anger and resentment the child feels toward the manipulating parent. After such badgering, he is likely to do one of two things. He may try to avoid contact with parents or he may try very hard to appease this parent. The latter is often an impossible feat. The child in this case suppresses his anger and resentment. He refuses to acknowledge his feelings because of the guilt that these feelings evoke. Such feelings often take an indirect form of passive aggressive behavior.

Three weeks later Todd's orchestra instructor asked Todd's mother not to attend practice. He had noticed that whenever she attended Todd performed very poorly. In family therapy, it was discovered that many of Todd's and his mother's problems were the result of passive aggressive behavior. Todd frequently did little things to irritate his mother, like making mistakes in practice, letting her dog get out of the house, knocking over various objects, and telling Dad when she made mistakes. Todd did not consciously realize that he was trying to get back at his mother; he thought that these were just accidents and, of course, some might have been.

Likewise, his mother was not aware of how she felt about herself, nor was she aware of how she manipulated those around her. This kind of interaction between parent and child tends to follow a vicious circle. Such indirect ways of communication are usually ineffective and destructive to relationships. The child who relies on such indirect means of relating to others will often behave this way throughout his life.

Effective Communication

Talking it Over

Before saying "no," it is often a good idea to talk over with the child *why* he wants what he is asking for. For example, if the child asks for a special notebook and you say "no," you may later have to give in when you get a note from his teacher saying that the students have to have that kind. It is also good to find out how much the thing he desires means to him. In another example, your son might ask for the car on Friday night. If you say "no" and then he informs you that his senior prom is that night, you may end up taking back the "no."

Recognizing His Feelings

In talking over the child's request, it is important to recognize and discuss his feelings. He may feel hurt, cheated, angry, or guilty. Discuss your own feelings with him as well. The following is an example of how feelings can become displaced:

Dicky: "I hate Tommy!"

Mom: "You are angry at your brother?"

Dicky: "No, I'm angry because he got a bicycle for Christmas and I didn't. You always have liked him better than me."

Mom: "You are angry at me and you feel cheated."

Dicky: "Yes, I guess so. I want a bicycle!"

Mom: "I didn't get you a bicycle because I felt that six years old was too young to have a bicycle. I was afraid you would get hurt. I know you feel bad about that. When you get older I will get you one too."

In this example, the child had not correctly identified his feelings. Had his mother not talked to him about his feelings, he might have gone on hating his brother. Had she scolded him for saying that he hated Tommy or was angry with her, he would have felt both guilty as well as cheated. In the example above, the child is still likely to feel some disappointment, but now he understands that his mother cares for him as well as his brother and his anger will diminish.

Alternatives

Talking over a child's request can also help the child come up with alternative ways of obtaining what he wants. If the item is costly, there may be some way he can earn the money. When the child invests his time and efforts to obtain a desired object, he will value it much more than if it was simply given to him. He will probably take much better care of what he has earned.

By encouraging the child to consider viable *alternatives,* we teach him problem solving skills which will help him deal with future frustrating situations. All of us have heard stories of famous individuals such as Helen Keller, Ray Charles, and Beethoven who have overcome tremendously frustrating handicaps. These individuals found ways around their misfortune. They did not get caught up in emotional self-pity or depression. The child who learns how to make the best of whatever happens has a much better chance of succeeding. Also, remember that talking it over is a means of discovering alternatives, not another chance for the child to talk you into letting him do what he wants.

Active Listening

In his book *Parent Effectiveness Training,* or PET for short, Dr. Thomas Gordon discusses the concept of active listening. This is a process whereby the listener is taught to check out the sender's message to make sure he has really understood how the speaker feels. Many misunderstandings occur because of poor communication. For example:

Jimmy: "I don't want to go to grandmother's house."
Dad: "There's something about going there that bothers you?"
Jimmy: "She always starts talking about what a cute baby I was."
Dad: "She embarrasses you so you don't want to go."
Jimmy: "I guess I could ask her not to talk about me that way."

Thus, active listening involves understanding the feeling which is being communicated and what the message really means. This is verified by rephrasing what was said in nonjudgmental terms so that the child can better hear himself or clarify his meaning. This is a difficult thing for individuals to do if they are used to being domineering and judgmental in their approach to others.

Some parents are unwilling to treat their children as thinking and feeling individuals and find it quite difficult to practice active listening initially. Like most behavior it takes a while to become accustomed to it, but the payoffs are the establishment of a more positive relationship and the elimination of a number of potential problems arising from misunderstanding.

Active listening is quite useful in helping individuals identify who owns the problem and finding problems. So if you are bothered by the kind of friends your child brings home, then you own the problem. If you are frustrated because someone is not paying attention to you, these are problems that you own. Acknowledging ownership in no way means that you do not care or are not concerned. The one who owns the problem is responsible for making others aware of his dissatisfaction.

When putting active listening into practice you must be careful not to manipulate the child in such a way that he feels compelled to conform to your solution to the problem. Such manipulation is usually viewed as a lack of acceptance and a threat to the child's independence.

I vs. You Messages

Another effective method of communication offered by Dr. Gordon involves the use of "I" messages as opposed to "you" messages. Dr. Gordon feels that parents speak differently to their children than they do to their adult friends. They tend to evaluate children's behavior, and thus create defensiveness by saying such things as, "look what you did," "it's your fault I've got troubles," "etc." He recommends that you use "I" messages with your children just as you do with other adults. "I" messages illustrate the impact the behavior is having on you and communicates your needs as a person, not as an authority. Examples of "I" messages include, "I don't feel like preparing lunch when I have to walk around toys on the floor," "I tend to get discouraged when I see my clean living room dirty again," and "I am very tired right now and I can not rest when someone is trying to pull me out of this chair."

According to Dr. Gordon, "I" messages are not limited to verbalizations but can be communicated to infants through nonverbal means. He believes that these nonverbal "I" messages are part of the bonding process that occurs between infant and caretaker. Effective communication should begin at infancy with the parent giving nonverbal acceptance cues such as smiling and holding the child. As the child matures, adults should communicate their concerns in a respectful manner, as though they were speaking to a friend rather than a servant.

No-Lose Approach

This approach, also suggested by Dr. Gordon (1975) is used to resolve conflict situations between parents and children. The parent directly involves the child in a joint search for a solution acceptable to both of them. After careful consideration of all possible alternatives, the child and parent agree to try a particular alternative. Since both have agreed to the solution, neither party is being forced to comply, no power is required and no resistance is encountered. Motivation to carry out the solution is high and a beneficial side-effect is that of developing problem solving skills in children. Dr. Gordon outlines the No-Lose Approach in six steps:

1. Identifying and defining the conflict.
2. Generating possible alternative solutions.
3. Evaluating the alternative solutions.
4. Deciding on the best acceptable solution.
5. Working out ways of implementing the solution.
6. Following up to evaluate how it worked.

Dr. Gordon cautions that you may initially encounter distrust, but this resistance will diminish as your children begin to trust your decision to abide by decisions arrived at jointly.

Family Communication

The words that family members speak change, but the unspoken process remains the same. The struggle of each member to maintain his role, with the attention and support that it affords, is continual. So, even though the content of arguments changes, the process is the same. Some individual members will argue to validate their intelligence while others fear domination. All of these struggles generally go on without individual family members being aware of the process, since each tends to focus on the content of the problems that are at issue. Therefore, similar problems and patterns continually arise unless family therapy or some drastic change, like the loss of a family member occurs.

Many disagreements will center around arguments regarding the family rules. Each member knows what's "ok and not ok" even though the rules may never have been stated clearly. Covert rules are often communicated by non-verbal movements of the body or tone of voice that are only meaningful to the immediate family. Indirect ways of communication are easily misinterpreted and can perpetuate troublesome family patterns of interaction. Even though unstated rules may continually cause distress and conflict they remain because they maintain a familiar balance among the members. The following are examples of rules which are often covert and may cause problems:

a. Don't discuss family problems with outsiders.
b. Don't mention Mother's drinking problem.
c. Affection is a sign of weakness and so we don't touch.

Symptoms such as those in a distressed child emerge as a way of handling relationships where incompatible definitions of rules exist (Haley, 1963). One individual symbolizes the distress of the whole family system. The distressed family then focuses on this one individual, called the "identified patient" by Virginia Satir (1964). The individual, often a child, allows himself to become the focus in order to distract the family from more serious difficulties which threaten to disrupt the family's togetherness. A child's bedwetting, excessive weight, asthma or acting out is often a symptom of poor relationships among members in general. In some cases, only methods such as family therapy, which improves family communication, clarifies rules, and restructures the interaction among family members will change the identified patient's behavior.

Communicating about the Birds and the Bees

Parents have been taught to think of educating their child about sex through a talk which is delivered before puberty. Dr. Ginott has suggested that it is much better to discuss sexual matters as opportunities arise in the child's daily life. TV shows and movies will often provide such opportunities.

The child will usually begin to ask questions about sex at a very young age. The answers to his questions should be in words which are appropriate to the child's age. The proper terms can, however, be used if you can give simple definitions. Answers need not be long or complicated. Many bookstores now carry very simple books on sexuality which can be of great help in explaining the "facts of life" to the young child.

If you find that you simply cannot talk about sexual matters in a calm matter of fact manner, these books will be of great help and perhaps you can find a school counselor or other family member to whom the child can direct his questions. It is much better to admit to the child that you have difficulty than to try and cover it up by telling him he is too young to know about such things. If he is left to his own devices to learn about sexual matters, he may get inaccurate information from friends or use his imagination to fill in what he doesn't know. Research has shown that adolescents who have accurate knowledge and healthy attitudes about sex are less likely to experiment in ways which will lead to serious problems.

Chapter 4

Early Social Learning and Development

Learning: A Definition

We cannot see learning as it occurs. It is a complex process which is hidden within our heads. We know that learning involves the firing of neurons and the storing of information but we only see the changes which occur in our behavior as we learn. Learning, then, can be defined as any relatively permanent change in behavior. We can say that weird Harold has learned to drive when he can keep his car on the road without accidents, or that Janie has learned to be afraid when she cries at the sight of a doctor. To say that learning has occurred, we must be able to observe that a relatively permanent change in behavior has occurred. It does not count if Ellen claims to know how to make friends; what's important is whether or not she talks and plays appropriately with other children.

So, learning and performance are not the same thing. Learning is necessary for one to perform well, but other things, like motivation, anxiety, and concentration are also important in determining how well one performs. If Ellen's mother spends so much time with her that she has no need of a friend, she will not be motivated to make friends. And if Johnny is anxious on tests, his performance may make him appear to be uninformed, when in fact, he really has learned the material. However, many children who are anxious about tests never learn the material because they feel anxious when they sit down to study and, thus, find lots of ways to avoid studying.

Three Ways to Learn

The developing child continuously faces environmental demands. The infant has few predetermined ways of dealing with the environment. He must *learn* to speak, to control his body, and even to tell right from wrong. He will learn what he needs to know through three processes. The first of these is called *operant conditioning** because as the child operates in the world, he learns from the consequences that occur as a result of that behavior. This type of learning is like the type discussed in chapter two. Another way the child can learn new ways of behavior is by watching what others do in similar situations and then *modeling* or *imitating* that behavior.

*The word conditioning means the same thing as learning.

This is learning without direct consequences. Consequences are involved only in the sense that the child is likely to have been positively reinforced for modeling the behavior of his caretakers. The third way in which children learn is called *classical conditioning* and it is the way he learns to be emotionally responsive to his environment. We will discuss each of these ways of learning separately, but you should keep in mind that they are complexly interwoven processes which are necessary for our survival.

Operant Conditioning

Initially, the infant may be seen as responsive to such basic environmental factors as warmth, contact, and nourishment. The infant's efforts are mostly directed toward obtaining these three *primary reinforcers*. These three primary reinforcers are thought to be basic for the survival of all newborn infants and hence are unlearned or innate.

As the child develops, he soon begins to associate the appearance of his parents with these primary reinforcers. The smiles on their faces and the sounds of their voices are paired many times with food, warmth, and contact. Parents then become very important to the infant as a result of their association with primary reinforcement. The infant will begin to cry out, not only when he is physically uncomfortable, but also for the company of his parents which is now positively reinforcing.

Environmental factors, like smiles and voices, which have become associated with primary reinforcers may be termed *secondary reinforcers*. They are learned and have acquired their reinforcing value through their association with primary (unlearned) reinforcers or with other well established secondary reinforcers. For example, clothing may become a secondary reinforcer of the child's dressing behavior through its association with warmth, a primary reinforcer. This association does not occur in warm areas of the world; so children in tropical areas do not find clothing reinforcing, and hence they wear none. Later, such things as money, thread, and washing powder become secondary reinforcers through their association with the secondary reinforcer, clothing. These things in and of themselves have little value to the infant, but through their association with the care of clothing to the infant, they will become important.

If you want to increase the value of some stimulus for a child, pair the stimulus with a primary reinforcer. That is why doctors give lollipops and dentists give balloons to child patients.

Modeling

Children are great imitators. Much of what they will learn in their life time is through observational learning.* It is indeed fortunate that we do not have to positively reinforce each of the thousands of new words and acts that a child will eventually acquire.

Children do not just model at random. According to Bandura (1966), whether they imitate a particular model or not is determined by a number of factors like the model's characteristics, the child's characteristics, and the child's expectations. Important characteristics of the model are nurturance (rewardingness), power and expertise, and similarity between the observer (child) and the model. So, most children are easily influenced by glamorous stars, sports heroes, peers who are similar, and nurturing, as opposed to cold and aloof parents. The child's characteristics, such as age, sex, and history of reinforcement are also important. For instance, imitation is increased when the child's efforts to be independent have often led to failure or when he has been punished frequently for acting independently. Children are more likely to model other children their own age. Boys more readily imitate aggressive models. From this information, certain practical information can be deduced. The friends with which a child plays will influence his behavior. The parent can help in such choices by pointing out to the child the good characteristics of the various individuals which the child admires. Don't use someone he thinks is "square" as an example or he will reject such behavior completely. Also, be careful not to create jealousy by saying something like "Why can't you be like Susie?" It is helpful to make sure the child plays with children of approximately the same age since the child may imitate inappropriate behavior of older or younger children. Children's imitation is increased when they see that the model is being rewarded and decreased if the model is punished. Therefore, whatever the child expects to happen as a result of imitating a model may have more influence on his behavior than the actual contingencies that exist (Bandura, 1965). Superstitious Stevey may buy a friend's lucky rabbit's foot with the idea that he can now pass his math test without studying.

Classical Conditioning of Emotions

Classical conditioning is a type of learning that deals with reflexive-like responses to external cues. (Pavlov, 1927) Most of the strong emotional and physiological feelings which we experience are learned through classical conditioning. Our positive feelings of love and happiness toward specific events or persons are conditioned responses which are learned, in part, through their

---

*Modeling, imitation, observational learning and vicarious conditioning all refer to the same process.

association with pleasantly exciting stimulus events. Our negative feelings of anger, fear, guilt, and depression are also reactions to specific events or persons. They have been acquired, in part, through association with traumatic stimulus events.

Our emotional feelings are often very subjective. We do not always know exactly why we feel the way we do. The situations in which the initial conditioning took place may have happened many years before but we still respond the same when faced with similar situations.

The following cases are examples of how classical conditioning of emotions occurs:

(1) Unrealistic Fears

When Mary was three years old, she fell into a swimming pool and almost drowned. Being under the water without air caused her to anxiously panic as she desperately tried to reach the surface. Whenever Mary sees a body of water she now feels very anxious. She will not go near water and insists on wearing water wings in the bathtub.

(2) Guilt

When Kip was ten years old, he was caught reading a *Playboy* magazine. His father lectured him on how he would go to Hell and then gave him a whipping. Kip felt very guilty about what had happened. Now, when he sees a *Playboy* magazine he gets that same guilty feeling. His stomach gets queasy, his hands sweat, and he feels very anxious.

Classical Conditioning: A Technical Explanation

A. In this learning process, a neutral stimulus is paired repeatedly with a stimulus which forces us to respond in some reflexive manner. It is called an unconditioned stimulus (US). The neutral stimulus eventually develops into a conditioned stimulus (CS) that when presented alone evokes a conditioned response (CR) which is very similar to the unconditioned response (UR) always elicited by the unconditioned stimulus.

B. If the conditioned stimulus is not again paired with the unconditioned stimulus, extinction will occur and the conditioned response will no longer be elicited by the conditioned stimulus.

C. Generalization will occur if the conditioned stimulus is similar to another conditioned stimulus. This second conditioned stimulus will then elicit the unconditioned response, but extinction usually occurs quickly.

D. An example of aversive classical conditioning of fear and its generalization:
  1. paired US (aversive noise) _____ UR (startled response)
     CS (motorcycle)
  2. later CS (motorcycle) _____ CR (startled response)
  3. still later CS_2 (bicycles) _____ CR (startled response)
E. The more often the pairing, the closer together the conditioned stimulus and unconditioned stimulus are in time the stronger is the conditioning and the more resistant a response is to extinction.
F. Aversive Classical Conditioning
  1. a. Before: A specific street intersection produces no special response.
     b. During: The street (CS) is paired with an accident (US) which produces fearful and anxious responses (UR).
     c. After: That street intersection (CS) alone now produces a fearful and anxious response (CR).
  2. a. Before: A school teacher with a ruler produces no special response.
     b. During: The teacher uses the ruler (US) to spank a child which produces a fearful and anxious response (UR).
     c. After: Now the sight of the teacher or ruler (CS) produces fear and anxiety (CR).

The Importance of Classical Conditioning

It is important for caretakers to understand how children develop emotional reactions because without this knowledge, one can mistakenly teach unhealthy emotional reactions or make light of fears that the child needs help overcoming. For example, every time Mr. Auther comes home his wife tells him all the things that Bobby has done and that he must paddle Bobby. The sight of his father now creates a terrible feeling of fear so Bobby hides whenever he hears his father approach. Similarly, the child who has a phobia*, such as the fear of dogs needs reassurance rather than criticism since such fears can worsen to the point that the child may become sick every time he goes anywhere that a dog could possibly be.

Extinguishing Inappropriate Reactions

One way to get rid of undesirable emotional responses is through the same process by which they were learned, classical conditioning. This time, however, we pair the stimulus which elicits the undesirable emotional response with a

*Phobia is an irrational fear.

situation that normally elicits a positive emotion. This is called *counter-conditioning.* So, now Bobby's father makes his mother take care of the discipline at the time of the misbehavior, and his father plays with Bobby when he comes home and occasionally brings a small surprise. The fear will extinguish and a positive emotion will replace it.

Another way to eliminate inappropriate emotional reactions with extinction is to find a way to get the child to experience a situation without having an extreme emotional reaction. For example, the little girl who is afraid of dogs may be perfectly fine around a puppy. As the puppy grows the child can adjust gradually and will eventually lose her fear. The child who is afraid of water can begin in the wading pool and slowly, over a number of sessions, be encouraged to feel comfortable in the larger pool. The key here is to find ways to prevent the extreme reaction while the child is in the presence of the feared stimulus. Thus, the child learns to respond to the stimulus in a more relaxed manner. The parent can also help by teaching the child how to reassure himself. Positive statements and instructions are best. Dwelling on the terrible things that might happen does not help.

Spontaneous Recovery

Sometimes, even after a conditioned emotional reaction has been extinguished, it will reoccur. This usually happens after a rest from the situation. The parent should not be surprised if next summer the child is again afraid of the water. Fortunately, when a behavior does spontaneously reoccur it is easier to extinguish than it was the first time.

Generalization of Conditioned Emotional Reactions

When a strong emotional reaction develops it can generalize to other stimuli that are similar in some way. In one case, a child was extremely jealous of her sister, whose pretty face captured everyone's attention in school. This child never got along with the girls who had pretty faces. She constantly strove to outdo them.

Generalization of conditioned fears can be serious. The child who gets into an embarrassing mess in a class at school may start out avoiding that class by going to the nurse everyday, finally refusing to go to any of his classes. When fears generalize, anything that reminds the child of the threatening situation will produce anxiety and fear. The child is then likely to avoid the situation and thereby gain positive reinforcement through anxiety relief. In some situations, it is best to require the child to face the threatening situation rather than avoid it so that extinction will occur.

**Learned Helplessness: A Theory Which Relates
to the Causes and Treatment of Depression,
Anxiety and Motivational Difficulties**

Seligman (1975) and several colleagues discovered learned help-lessness in the course of their investigation of the effects of fear on dogs. They restrained dogs in a box and exposed them to a series of tones, each followed by a shock. The dogs could do nothing but whimper and struggle; they were in an *uncontrollable* situation.

After this, each dog was placed in a two-sided chamber in which he could escape shock by simply jumping from one side to the other. He could avoid shock altogether if he jumped as soon as he heard the tone. A normal dog soon learns to avoid shock and will leisurely jump back and forth thousands of times without being shocked. In fact, a normal dog may never find out that the experimenter has turned off the shock and continues his well-learned habit for no reason.

It was Seligman's intention to teach the dogs which he had re-strained and shocked to become good at avoiding shocks in the two-sided box. To his surprise, most of these dogs just ran around a little, whimpered, and finally lay down. Two-thirds never learned to jump to avoid the shock; they just laid there and did nothing to relieve their pain.

Changes in the helpless dogs' personalities outside the box were noted. Helpless dogs seemed to wilt when handled, becoming totally submissive, whereas non-helpless dogs resisted handling and ran to the backs of their cages to avoid the experimenter.

Similar results have been found with many other species, including man. Experiments with humans have shown that three factors pro-duce learned helplessness, (1) the laboratory experience of uncon-trollability ("nothing I do will count"), (2) being told that chance, rather than skill, determines the outcome, and (3) the viewpoint that good things in life come to one by luck, not effort.

Any or all three of the above factors will lead to the subject's inability to learn to respond adaptively to difficulty. These three fac-tors all *lessen motivation* by contributing to the belief or *expectation* that responding and relief are independent.

Humans who have come to perceive their environment as uncon-trollable say such things as "why should I try, it won't make any difference. Things just don't work out for me. I have rotten luck."

Helplessness also inhibits normal aggression and defensive re-sponses. Dogs who had previously received inescapable shock lost out in competition for food when competing with dogs who had been able to escape shock. In humans, helplessness is exhibited in such attitudes as "why try for that job, I could never really land a good position" or "It won't do any good to say anything about it, that would only make things worse."

Helplessness also inhibits resolution of problems. People who were given unsolvable problems to work first, were later unable to work several problems that most people who had not experienced the unsolvable problems could readily solve.

In prolonged studies with animals in uncontrollable stress situations, drastic changes in health and personality have been observed. These include ulcers, weakness, irritability, depression, bizarre behaviors, unpredictability, poor grooming habits, sleep disturbance, emotional outbursts, and many others.

Perceiving our environment as uncontrollable is then a major factor contributing to depression, lack of assertiveness, health problems, problem-solving difficulties, and lack of motivation.

It has also been discovered that *uncontrollable* reward impairs adaptive learning in a similar way. Animals given free food in pretraining later fail to learn to push a bar to get food. They just sat around, waiting for food to be dropped in and never learned to push the bar. Similar studies have shown that helplessness experiences reduce competitiveness.

This kind of apathy has been labeled the "spoiled brat" or learned indolence syndrome. In humans, we can see similar behavior in people who receive welfare for prolonged periods or in the person who gets everything he wants because of some uncontrollable factor such as physical beauty. The latter individual has trouble finding meaning in life. No matter what he does, people are still attracted to him. What he does appears not to matter. He is loved not for his actions but for his appearance. Similarly, the person who finds that he has finally reached his life's goal may experience a great letdown because of the feeling that he doesn't have to strive any more. Thus, uncontrollability explains the occurrence of suicide and depression among those who appear to have a lot going for them.

Man's tendency to generalize from one situation to another is probably responsible for the widespread effect of the helpless experience. When we find that we are helpless in some situation at some particular time in our lives we let that feeling generalize to other times and similar situations. We begin to believe that relief is independent of our actions. It is a "what can I do about it" feeling or a "life's not fair" response. In such cases, the environment has not taught us to deal adaptively with frustration. We have unrealistic expectations that life is fair, when it is not; or that trying really hard *should* lead to success, when it doesn't always. And so we become disappointed, depressed and helpless too easily.

Thus, the two major consequences of experiences with uncontrollable events are lack of motivation and difficulty in believing that a response can be effective (uncontrollability distorts *perception of control*). We have not effectively discriminated between situations where our actions count and ones in which there really is no hope beyond luck.

Innoculating your child against learned helplessness will involve helping him to discriminate between those situations where he can have effect and those that he will not be able to change.

One final concept is important in understanding how to *prevent* learned helplessness—the concept of behavioral immunization. Seligman discovered that dogs, who first learned to jump to escape shocks before being restrained and shocked, later returned to effective performance in the jumping box. They had become immune to helplessness. The implications for humans are clear. Those who have learned that they can be effective, though life is hard and there are disappointments, will be more resistant than those who have had nothing but success or those for whom life has been so bewildering that it is hard for them to believe that anything they do will matter. The former will give up easily when faced with frustration, while the latter may not try at all. Immunizing a child consists of reinforcing all the times when his efforts did make a difference and finding situations in which he is quite likely to feel effective.

The Caretaker as a Teacher

For the child to learn quickly, the caretaker should provide an orderly and consistent set of cues*, at a time when the child is paying attention. The child must be able to discover what relationships exist between the cues and what behaviors will effect changes in these relationships.

To facilitate learning, the caretaker should use a calm, patient voice, being careful to convey support and confidence, i.e. "place the plates carefully on the first shelf of this cabinet," not "I want this done right and you better not break a single plate." Instructions should be positively worded, such as, "Work carefully so that everything stays upright," not "Don't spill that now!" In looking at the way the last sentence is worded, you will note that the last three words the child hears is the command "spill that now." Similarly, the coaches often make the mistake of saying, "Don't drop the ball" instead of, "Your

---

*Cues-commands, signs, or signals.

hands are going to grip that ball like they had super glue on them." Finally, keep instruction sessions short and fun. If you cannot teach the child without getting into an emotional battle find someone else to instruct the child and watch what he does and says. You can learn to be a good teacher. Being a good teacher however, takes patience and skill.

Chapter 5

Emotional Reactions

Signs of Stress and Anxiety

Emotional reactions occur in situations which are perceived by the individual as being confusing, threatening, tragic, or frustrating. Overt signs of emotional stress may include restlessness, irritability, wrinkling of the brow, nail biting, inappropriate eating habits, crying, and sudden unexplained changes in behavior. Within the body, many other changes occur as a result of emotional stress. These include constriction of blood vessels, a slowing down of the digestive processes, increased heart rate, adrenalin production, anxiety, and perspiration. If the individual remains emotionally distressed for long periods of time these physiological changes can result in actual damage to the body. Such problems as headaches, phlebitis, arthritis, ulcers, high blood pressure, acne, and colitis are now thought to be related to emotional stress.

Emotional reaction to environmental demands has been a prerequisite for survival throughout the ages. The survival of primitive man depended on the ability to strike out violently and be vigilant when in a dangerous environment. Those who failed to become anxious, irritable, or fearful at appropriate times probably starved to death or became dinner for some better adapted creature.

Today, even though there are fewer direct threats to our life, the ability to react emotionally is still important. For example, if we are walking in the street and see a car coming at us, adrenalin begins to flow, our heart beats faster, and we become fearful. This enables us to think and move faster in order to avoid tragedy.

On the other hand, our emotional nature can also cause problems. It is no longer functional to meet many of today's stressful situations with primitive emotional reactions. Therefore, if the guy at the diner says that it is closing time after you have waited 30 minutes to order, knocking him in the head and taking his food is not a feasible solution. What usually occurs today is that we become very angry and/or depressed over such events. These emotional reactions can stay with us long after we have forgotten what made us feel this way. So we may find ourselves kicking the dog and taking our frustrations out on our spouse that evening. The consequences for such aggressive behaviors may be that our spouse and dog will learn to avoid us. If we tend to hold back our emotions, *acting* as though nothing bothers us, we may end up with ulcers, migraine headaches, or some other physical symptoms of our distress. But these consequences are not as drastic or immediate as are those for "doing in" the guy at the diner. This type of delayed emotional reaction is sometimes called displaced agression.

The problem, then, is that we often overreact and allow emotional feelings to stay with us long after the events which initiate them. As parents, we can help our children learn to deal more assertively and less emotionally with situations which involve frustration, fear, and sorrow. The following discussions will illustrate how this can be accomplished.

Frustration and Emotion

Emotional responses which occur in response to frustrating situations are by far the most common. From his birth a child constantly meets situations which limit his freedom. He feels frustrated when he is told that he cannot play outside, or when he finds that he is not physically able to get the top off a candy jar, or that the other kids won't play with him. These disappointments often result in emotional reactions and the signs of stress described earlier.

Crying is the first observable emotional response an infant makes. Being brought forth into this world in a violent manner from a warm, comfortable environment generally elicits crying and this remains a primary way of communicating discomfort for many months. The infant quickly learns that crying is usually followed by primary reinforcement. As the parents become more important through their association with satisfaction of basic needs, the child may begin to cry for attention even though he is not physically uncomfortable. If the child learns that someone will come running each time he cries (i.e. he is reinforced for crying), we can predict that the frequency of crying will increase. In some cases, the infant's crying may increase dramatically. Such a demanding child can be very distressing and disturbing to the parents. It may appear to them that the child is emotionally upset or unhappy much of the time. Most parents get wise to the infant's fake crying act and ignore him when they are sure that all the child wants is more attention. Crying for attention will then decrease, and this behavior is said to extinguish. Hopefully, the child will learn to accept that others cannot always wait on him. Eventually, he will learn constructive ways of getting attention such as drawing a picture or learning a piano selection.

In Chapter Two, we illustrated that the extinction procedure is helpful in dealing with the "Mommy may I" syndrome. When the caretaker is consistent in decisions about what the child can do, the child learns that his tantrums are useless. The child who gets everything he demands, and attention whenever he wants is usually labeled "spoiled." These children are often very emotional. They are rarely happy with anyone or anything.

When the spoiled child is told that he can't have something he wants, he often reacts in the same manner as he did when he was an infant and was uncomfortable. He rages, flails his arms, and cries very loudly. After all, these behaviors worked to get what he wanted before, so he continues in the same manner. When parents give in to this inappropriate behavior and let the child have his way, they reinforce this emotional behavior. We can predict, then, that the frequency and severity of these emotional tantrums will increase. The word "no" becomes a cue for a tantrum.

If tantrums are not extinguished, (i.e. the child does not learn to accept that others will not always fulfill his expectations) the child may develop emotional problems in later life. The spoiled child may become the incorrigible teenager who can't understand why he can't have a new car or stay out all night. The teenager's response to this frustrating situation may be seen as similar to childhood tantrums, though far more destructive. He may become angry with his parents or steal a car or run away from home.

Such common human emotions as anger, depression, and pouting may be seen as resulting in part from the early reinforcement of emotional behavior. It is not necessary to deprive a child of things he wants just to avoid having a "spoiled child." The point here is that when you say "no" you mean no. In this way, you are not reinforcing inappropriate emotional behavior; you are helping him learn early that it is not always possible to have everything his way.

Fear

Fear is an emotion which can result from direct physical threat, but usually children's fears center around fantasy, guilt, loss of love, loss of security, or loss of self concept.

The child's self concept is based on the image they have of themselves as a person. The child's image of himself can be hurt by failure and criticism. Excessive amounts of either may lead the child to conclude that he is worthless, ugly, or unwanted. He may become anxious, defensive, insecure, and fearful of further loss as a result. Fear of failure and learned helplessness are often characteristic of children with low self-concepts. Fear of loss of security generally involves uncertainty, indefiniteness, and change. Most children feel secure in a constant and predictable environment. Just changing the furniture around in a room can be disturbing to a child. The very insecure child may develop a compulsive need to have each object in its place and each person in his proper role.

Sources of Fear

Physical Support

One of the few things young infants fear is loss of physical support. If the infant is not held securely, he will certainly let you know about it. Most amusement park rides are not for infants and young children. Early scares from rides or accidental falls are probably responsible for many adults' fear of heights and airplanes.

Financial Security

The child is dependent upon the parent for food, clothes, shelter, etc. Excessive financial worries may make the child feel insecure and fearful for his future. The following case will illustrate: Mr. and Mrs. Tight talked incessantly about the cost of living. Mrs. Tight would say such things as "I just know we are all going to end up in the poor farm. I don't know where our next meal is coming from. The kids eat so much, I can hardly keep food in the house. If we had to see a doctor, I don't think we could pay him."

Their eight year old son, Charlie became very concerned about this. He began eating less to save them money and so he lost a good deal of weight. About the same time, he began to have pains in his side but he told no one for fear that they would have to pay a doctor. At Easter time, he was rushed to the hospital for an emergency appendectomy. His recovery was complicated because he had not been eating properly.

Mr. and Mrs. Tight have since discovered that they shouldn't talk about financial worries in front of the kids. As you may have guessed, this couple had plenty of money in the bank, but little Charlie didn't know this. He really believed that they were all going to the poor farm.

Whether a child is secure and satisfied in his home may depend on how he compares his situation with that of his friends. If his parents drive a year-old Ford and everybody else's parents have new Cadillacs, he may feel poor and ashamed. A child's view of the world is often restricted to his immediate environment. It may be hard for him to grasp that 5/6th of the people in the world have no car at all. He may also find it hard to believe that other children wouldn't like him any better if his parents had a new car.

It is important, then, that parents begin early in teaching the child to feel lucky to be who he is and have what advantages he has. If, however, we as parents are dissatisfied with our lot in life, such tactics as telling the child to think of the poor children in India and be "glad" may not be very convincing.

Divorce

Another source of fear and insecurity for the child can come out of parents' marital problems. Marital conflict is generally very stressful for the child. He may often be drawn into fights and feel forced to choose between one side or the other. His parents may try to win his affection by belittling each other or by doing special favors for the child. In such situations, the child may learn that he can get whatever he wants by playing one parent against the other, which only serves to stir up more anger and resentment. The child who must live in such a hostile atmosphere is likely to feel confused and insecure. He does not know who to believe or what will happen next since the two people who are supposed to guide and protect him cannot seem to cope with their own lives.

Marital problems do not always have to have such a destructive effect on the child. Parents who can argue and come to constructive solutions, as a result, need not worry about disagreeing in front of the children. When parental arguments tend to lead to name calling, physical struggles, and no constructive solution, they are better held at times when the child is not present. In spite of their differences, it is important for parents to provide a united front when it comes to disciplinary measures. This way, neither parent becomes the villain or the saint.

Communication is essential when parents are considering divorce. It is important that parents find out what their children are thinking. The following example will illustrate how the child can misunderstand what is happening. Anne was five years old when her parents started to have problems. There was much bitterness between them at this time. Her grandmother told her that her father had found someone to *replace* her mother. Annie became very fearful of and angry with her father. She imagined that her father was going to make her mother disappear completely, so that she would no longer exist.

Such misgivings on the part of the child could be avoided with a few long talks. The child should be told what changes might occur if their parents get a divorce. Such knowledge often helps eliminate some of the indefiniteness and uncertainty that generates feelings of insecurity at such times.

Fantasy

Fears related to fantasy are very common among children and it is not hard to see why. The young child is small and helpless in this world. He has a very incomplete view of the world. When he does not have a ready answer, he may incessantly question his parents or make things up to fill in these information gaps. Not knowing, as we have seen before, can be stressful.

Television appears to have become one of children's major sources of "gap filling." This can be positive, in that the child can see and experience things he would never have known about. Unfortunately many of the programs which children watch can produce fear. After watching the Hairy Swamp Monster eat fifty people on TV, it is not surprising to find that a child has nightmares and no longer wants to play at the creek.

As a parent, you can do two things to try to lessen the effects of scary TV shows. You can forbid the child to watch them and try to make sure that he will not see them when he visits other homes. We recommend that if you try this approach, you gradually remove these restrictions as he becomes older since his friends will all be watching scary TV programming and it will be hard to enforce such rules. You may, however, be surprised to find that he has internalized your values, and does not care to watch scary programs.

The other thing that you can do is explain to the child at a very young age that these monsters are not real, never have been, and never will be. You may have to go to great lengths to convince the child that the blood and costumes are fake. A trip through a movie studio might be most helpful.

A few people never grow out of these fears. They are always anxious and fearful that some supernatural event is going to happen. They supply the fortune tellers, exorcists, and psychologists with a steady business.

Guilt

Guilt is an emotional reaction in which the individual is fearful of punishment by either man or God. The child first learns what is "wrong" from those around him. When he misbehaves or even thinks about misbehaving in a way which he knows will be punished, he feels anxious (or guilty). Thus, we can say that guilt is an emotional reaction which anticipates punishment. The way in which the caretaker punishes will determine how guilt prone the child becomes. The child who does *not* learn what others consider to be wrong and, who is rarely corrected, may not experience any guilt for acts which others consider antisocial. The child who is taught what is wrong, but is rarely corrected, may feel guilty but won't change his antisocial behavior. The child who learns that many things he does are wrong, and who is excessively punished for them, will usually follow a narrow path. This child feels guilt even when he has bad thoughts or dreams. The following case will illustrate how this can happen.

Virginia's parents were very religious so she attended a Christian school for girls. When she was nine, she heard a priest lecture on the evils of masturbation. In his fire and brimstone manner, he conveyed the message that the human body was unclean and that those who engaged in this act would perish in Hell.

Virginia became very fearful. She realized that she had touched herself in this manner and decided never to touch her genital area again. About this time, her brother was caught masturbating. He was severely disgraced. She knew that other people touched themselves and she feared touching things that they touched because they were unclean. She spent much time washing her hands and anything else other people had touched. Needless to say, her cat got tired of being washed and began hiding when she approached with the wash pail.

Virginia was seen by a psychologist following her marriage at age twenty. She could not adjust to married life. She could not bear the thought of sex. She couldn't even allow a doctor to examine her. She spent most of her time washing her hands and cleaning where others had touched. She had a very low opinion of herself as a person and felt that she was unclean, even though she had done nothing to support this idea.

Another reaction to a strict upbringing can be seen in "good" individuals who periodically act out of character, that is, they may take drugs, skip school, or act promiscuously. Such individuals try to be very good, but are bored and often depressed as a result of self-denial. These individuals periodically "act out" in protest, trying to find some excitement to relieve their depression. They soon begin to feel guilty over what they have done and become even more depressed. This cycle usually repeats itself many times throughout their lives.

It is not necessary, then, to induce fear of God or man to cause the child to act appropriately. This type of procedure has many side effects as the previous example has shown. The key is to follow desired behavior with positive consequences and undesired behavior with mild aversive consequences. There is little need to use anger, hostility, or "God's going to get you" tactics.

Fear of Failure

The child who perceives that he has failed to perform well, will often react emotionally. We say "perceive" because failure is relative to an individual's past history of reinforcement. This involves his self-image, his expectations, and the pressure placed on him by others. The following cases are illustrative of how failure is relative.

Case 1: Percy, whiz kid and class genius, always thought of himself as infallible. He never made anything but A's until his senior year. His parents always bragged about his grades and were planning to send him to Harvard. During his senior year, he made a C and became extremely depressed. Percy felt that he was a failure. He felt that he had let everyone down. He spent three months in a psychiatric hospital after which he never returned to school.

Case 2: Easy going Eddie usually makes D's and F's. On his last report card, he dropped from a D in math to an F but neither he nor his parents noticed this drop because they couldn't remember what he made last time. When asked if he feels he is a failure, Eddie doesn't know why anyone would ask.

Sometimes a child's reaction to failure may not be overtly observable, even though he may be experiencing guilt, anxiety, and self-doubt. Failure can be seen as a frustrating and punishing experience for most children. The following statements are typical of children's responses to failure situations.

(1) "I don't think I want to play hockey anymore because I miss cartoons on T.V. Anyway, the coach is goofy."

(2) "I don't want to go to Boy Scouts anymore because nobody there is my friend."

(3) "I'm not taking Linda to the prom because she's going with Herby Hero. I don't even like her anyway, she's too snobby."

These statements usually mean the child is denying or rationalizing away the hurt in order to defend himself from loss of face. The wise parent will sense this hurt and talk it out with the child. The best way to begin is to find out exactly what it is about the situation which is causing him to avoid it (i.e. what is punishing to the child?). Sometimes you can check with others, like the scout leader or the coach, to determine this because the child may not want to tell, or he may not be aware of his own hurt feelings. For example: Butch isn't getting along with the other boy scouts and wants to drop out. His mom finds out that he puts all the other kids down and they in turn exclude him from the clique because of his behavior. The boy scout leader feels that Butch isn't aware that his "put downs" really hurt the other children's feelings.

If his mom lets him drop out, she will reinforce his copping out of social situations. We might then predict that Butch's frequency of avoiding people will increase. The best thing for her to do is to help him understand how others feel when they are insulted, and to use a reinforcement program to improve his social skills. Such programs are discussed in Chapter 10.

However, there will be times that dropping out of situations is the best thing for the child. When the child is not prepared, or physically not ready to compete, then it might be best if the child found some other interest. For example: Mary wanted to become a shoe model so she took all kinds of lessons and looked everywhere for a job. She, however, wore a size 10 shoe D width and so, no one would consider her for a job. She became depressed and sensitive about her feet. Her mother realized this and decided to get her interested in working with handicapped children. Mary has received much recognition for her work and she doesn't remember why she wanted to model shoes.

Fear, Failure and Performance

If the child is trying to learn a complex task such as ice skating, tumbling, or algebra, repeated failure may result in tears, anger, anxiety, and the other accompanying emotional reactions which result from frustration. When the

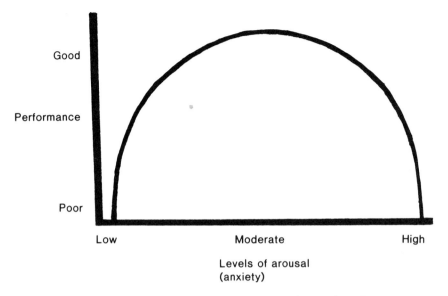

Figure 6. Graph of the relationship between anxiety and performance.

child is nervous his performance may get worse instead of improving. The more he doubts his ability, the less clearly he thinks and the more anxious he becomes. Anxiety and performance are known to work as shown on the above graph.

As you can see from the graph, some failure or chance of failure can be motivating. However, when the task is too easy the child is likely to become bored. If the task is too hard the child may become disinterested or emotional. He will end up hating that activity.

Fear of Failure and Loss of Self Esteem

Repeated failure in the child's life may result in a loss of self esteem and a fear of new situations. In such cases, the child begins to doubt his ability and adequacy. He may shy away from future situations where failure and loss of face may occur. The following statements, though intended to improve the child's behavior, may only cause them to further withdraw from competition:

(1) "Why can't you be like other kids and participate in sports? I think you're lazy."
(2) "You're the clumsiest girl I ever saw. Why can't you be dainty like your sister?"
(3) "Hush up! You talk and talk but don't even know anything about what you are saying."

Competition and Jealousy

Competition can motivate children to improve their performance. If, however, too much emphasis is placed on being the "best," many emotional side effects will result. Competition can set children against each other and foster jealousy. In such situations, children may be hesitant to help one another and even try to keep others from achieving as the following example will show: Mary always won the weekly spelling bee gold star. The teacher liked to talk about how gifted she was and scolded the rest of the class for being such dummies. One day Mary missed school and so she asked her best friend, Jane, to bring her that week's spelling words. Jane wanted very badly to win the spelling bee so that the teacher would not think she was dumb. She resented Mary's winning and so she gave her a list with four misspelled words.

This kind of situation usually happens when only a few can receive the prize. In the above example, it might be better for the teacher to give each child a gold star when they could spell each word correctly. In this way, everybody learns all the words at their own pace and is reinforced for their achievement.

Parents often unknowingly foster rivalries between brothers and sisters by comparing their accomplishments. Such comparison is best avoided because the child who feels he is the loser may drop out of competition and become the rebellious "black sheep" of the family.

Competition is usually not detrimental when a child competes to better his own performance or to achieve a common group goal. In the latter case, the child learns to work with others for the benefit of all. This quality is necessary if a society is to survive.

Rejection

Children also become fearful when they face rejection. This involves the threat of loss of love by a parent or other valued person. Sometimes children fear that their parents will reject them if they fail to live up to their parents' ideals. Thus, the boy who finds he did not make the soccer team may try to hide this fact or lie about why he's not participating. The key here is to convey to the child that he is loved as a person and not for what he's accomplished. The child must feel that his parents like him to do well for his own sake, not theirs.

Some parents make the mistake of trying to use their love to control their children's behavior. The following examples will illustrate.

(1) "Don't do that again, Bobby; Mother doesn't love little boys who act like that."

(2) "Jr., we really hope you will go to medical school and be the kind of son that we can be proud to say is our own. We don't want you to get married like that useless brother of yours."

These types of tactics put a lot of pressure on the child to conform. Too often, they backfire about the time of adolescence. The child may declare that he wants to be accepted the way he is and not because he is a football star or straight A student. He may rebel doing just the opposite of what his parents wanted in an effort to achieve recognition as a person. At this point, there is not much a parent can do to control the adolescent's behavior.

Communication between the parent and youth can help, if done correctly. This involves the parent finding out what the youth believes without passing any judgment on the issues. The parents can then express their beliefs and why they feel as they do without belittling the youth. Statements such as those below only make matters worse:

(1) "People will think you are one of those pinko fags with your hair as long as it is."
(2) "I'm not going to let you go around smoking pot and having people think you're a hippie."
(3) "An atheist! Nonsense! You don't know what you are. I'll tell you what you are. . . !"

Simply asking the youth to improve his behavior as a favor to you, or because you will feel more comfortable, is likely to get better results. Be sure and thank him for any small improvements.

Health Fears

Emotional reactions can result from the child's excessive concern for his health, or that of his parents. It is wise to avoid too much talk about germs and diseases. The following statements may generate much anxiety and still not result in the desired response:

(a) "I think your cousin Alfred must have gotten that disease that killed him from playing in the grass. You shouldn't play in the grass like he did."
(b) "Take your vitamin pills or you will get scurvy and rickets. What's the matter with you? Do you want your bones to be brittle and your skin to be scaly?"
(c) "I don't want you around those kids on the corner because they probably have lice and all kinds of diseases. You know their parents don't take them to church."
(d) "I hate for you to go to school when all those other kids are sick. You'll probably get sick too and then I'll get sick also."
(e) "Did you hear all about what they did to Mrs. Crank when they took out her gallstones! Well, first. . . ."

Statements (a), (b), and (c) are attempts at correcting behavior. The child, however, may see that these lines of reasoning are faulty and consequently ignore the warnings. In case (a) it is easy for them to see that all children play in the grass and do not die from it. Likewise, the child can see that other people who don't take vitamin pills are healthy. It may also be obvious to the child that his friends on the corner don't have lice (c).

Even though these statements may not overtly change the child's behavior, they may still create anxiety and worry. When a child becomes worried and anxious about sickness, he may become fatigued. Such exhaustion may actually make him more vulnerable to disease.

While it is good for children to have a realistic view of medical problems, excessive discussion can be fear producing. When discussion of such problems (for example (e)), goes into all the gory details, the child, or anyone else for that matter, may feel anxious and fear for his own health. The child may develop an excessive fear of doctors and hospitals. To get the child to take care of himself, simply reinforce cleanliness and good eating habits with praise. Make him feel good about himself and his body and he will take good care of himself.

Grief

In our culture grief is the usual reaction to the loss of a cherished person. The individual is likely to have feelings of anger, aloneness, and despair. There is no set reaction to death and individuals will vary considerably in their reactions. Certain cultures teach that death is a time to celebrate the person's passing on to the great spirit and some religions encourage such faith that the family's suffering may be lessened considerably.

The child's reaction to the loss of a loved one will be influenced greatly by what he has learned about death and the age of the child at the time of the loss. In her book *On Death and Dying,* Elizabeth Kubler-Ross (1969) discusses the importance of the child's age. The young toddler generally reacts with distress to being separated from the loved person. As the child becomes more mobile he also becomes concerned about mutilations, especially if he has seen animals along the road that have been disfigured. At around five years of age, death is like a bogey man that comes and takes people away. Only around the ages of 9 or 10 does the child begin to think of death as a permanent biological process. Children react differently to the loss of loved ones (Kubler-Ross, 1969). Some cry and become depressed while others appear not to be affected at all. Some refuse to believe and may have to be reminded occasionally that that which they cherished is really gone. They may lose their appetite, have insomnia, become irritable and withdrawn. The child's reaction to the loss of a cherished person is a complex mixture of emotional feelings. One emotion is that of frustration in that the child can not have the person he once loved. He can no longer experience what he once had. It is up to the parents to help the child learn to accept his loss and recover quickly.

The child who grows up on the farm is probably much better able to withstand the loss of a loved one. This child is likely to have witnessed the death and birth of many animals. He is likely to have the realistic view that life is temporary and he has a feeling of being part of a universal cycle.

The child who has had many pets may also have a similar advantage since pets invariably die. The wise parent can point out to the remorseful child that their pet led a good life and had a good home. The child can be helped to understand that nature keeps itself in balance by a continuous process of giving and taking. There must be room for the new born. Replacing the pet can help, but isn't necessary.

The child or adult who has not been prepared to deal with such losses may go into long periods of depression and grief following the loss of a loved one. They may refuse to believe that the person is actually dead and may continue to act as if he were alive. Some professionals feel that it is important that the child attend the funeral so that he will understand that the loved one is gone and will not return.

Extreme reactions can occur if the child has been told unrealistic things about death. Such things as people go to sleep for a long time or even that they go to live in a nice place can be harmful. The young child who is told this may become very angry with the one who has died. He may feel deserted and rejected because the deceased won't wake up and come back. He may even do as one child did, and try to wake the deceased up at the funeral.

Such extreme reactions may also occur when guilt is involved. The child who feels he has in some way mistreated or caused the death of a loved one may become very anxious and remorseful. He feels unfinished in that he would like to say he didn't mean it, but the person is gone. He may even fear retribution from the deceased loved one. The parent can help by reassuring the child that the loved one knew that the child meant no harm.

Communications such as these between parent and child are very important at such times. The child should be allowed to vent his emotional feelings to someone who is understanding. Keeping in these feelings and misconceptions of death can lead to later emotional disturbance (Kubler-Ross, 1969).

In summary, we can see that it is important for the child to have someone with whom he can communicate his feelings and from whom he can obtain realistic, soothing explanations. Finally, it is best if the parents can help the child recover quickly from his grief. This involves diverting his attention to other activities and encouraging him to resume his life rather than allowing him to grieve excessively.

Chapter 6

Early Development of the Child

The Unborn Child

The unborn child (fetus) develops during a nine month period in a warm, dark, liquid environment. Its well being is totally dependent on its mothers health. The mother's diet provides the unborn child with its sole source of nourishment. The wise mother should seek advice about nutrition very early during pregnancy. THE EARLY MONTHS ARE THE MOST CRITICAL. Studies have shown that vitamins are of crucial importance during the early months. Too few vitamins or excesses can result in permanent damage to the child.

The pregnant mother should avoid all drugs except those prescribed by her doctor. Such common drugs as caffeine, nicotine, alcohol, aspirin, and tranquilizers are known to affect the fetus and are thought to cause birth defects. The fetus can also become addicted to drugs. Children born to heroin addicts go through withdrawal at birth and may die if proper medical help is not available.

The pregnant mother should be especially careful to avoid exposing herself to contagious diseases. Diseases such as German measles, venereal diseases, and some types of influenzas can detrimentally affect the fetus. The pregnant mother should consult her doctor before taking any drug or if she contacts any serious illness.

The Fetus That Learns

No one knows exactly what the fetus experiences or learns in its dark and sublime environment. There is research, however, to indicate that the fetus is capable of learning. Evidently, it is aware of sounds and can be taught to respond to changes in its environment through classical condition procedures like those described in chapter four.

We know that the mother's health and diet are important, but what about the mental health of the mother? If she is anxious, fearful, or upset, does the fetus experience these emotional responses and learn them from her? The answers to these questions are not yet available, but there is evidence to suggest that the fetus is affected by the mother's mental state as well as her health. She might do well to seek aid from a psychologist or other professional if she becomes anxious and worried.

During the birth process, the child is propelled from its secure environment in an abrupt way. Doctors in the past have generally slapped the helpless infant on the rear and sent it to the nursery. A French obstetrician, Frederick Le Boyer (1975), now believes that this is an inappropriate way to welcome the new infant into the world. He feels that this procedure is traumatic for the newborn infant. He has developed a delivery method which requires that the delivery room be dim and quiet. The infant is not slapped and the mother is allowed to hold the baby for awhile. This method has been well received by many psychologists, but some obstetricians think that it is unnecessary. This theory has received some support (Trotter, 1977), but other findings have been negative (Nelson, *et. al.*, 1980). If you like this idea, you may have to look for awhile to find a doctor who will use the Le Boyer method to deliver your baby.

The Le Boyer method involves natural childbirth, which means that the mother is not anesthetized during labor. Natural childbirth has several advantages, one being the absence of drugs which affect the infant and make it sluggish during the first few days of life. Another advantage is that the mother sometimes feels more fulfilled and satisfied if she can see the child when it is born.

Some hospitals now allow the father to be present in the delivery room during the birth process. Many psychologists believe that this joint experience brings the two parents closer together and increases the father's interest in his baby. This joint family experience is called bonding and recent research has suggested that it may enhance the overall family relationship.

At birth, the new infant reflexively roots and sucks in search of food for survival. It may sleep as much as twenty hours a day for the first three weeks of life. It is relatively insensitive to external pain, but it is well in tune with internal changes such as hunger or colic. Otherwise, it is helpless. Its ability to interpret what it hears, sees, and smells is very limited. Its movement is restricted to turning its head and thrashing with its arms and legs. It cannot move itself about and so it should be turned occasionally to insure comfort. The infant cannot move away from harmful objects such as plastic bags. Sharp objects or small objects which might be swallowed must not be allowed near the infant. Individuals who have colds should be asked to wait until they are better to see the baby. The infant, however, need not be secluded and sheltered from noise and people. It is not as fragile as its small size might lead you to believe and will benefit from the stimulation of new sounds and sights as long as they are not too disturbing. It will enjoy being carried about and rocked in almost anyone's arms. It will, however, protest if not supported firmly. Sudden changes downward, even though it is not really falling, will bring startled cries from the infant. Loud noise also produces a startled response in the infant. Later, at about six months, it will begin to react to strangers. Its senses are not well enough developed to tell caretakers from visitors. It will invariably prefer the former and may reject new faces for many months.

Figure 7 indicates the order and months at which basic skills are likely to develop. Each infant is unique and thus developmental patterns differ for each infant. You should not become concerned if the infant does not pull itself up by 12 months of age nor should you try to force behaviors to occur. If the infant is pushed too hard the relationship between you and your child may suffer. This caretaker-child relationship is much more important than the number of skills the infant has developed. It is better, then, to occasionally encourage these tasks, avoiding long, drawn out, emotional sessions.

As the child matures, many of the simple skills listed below will spontaneously occur as a result of maturation. This means that the child's muscles and perceptual abilities have developed to the point that he is able to perform the skill. More complex skills will occur only after the child has matured and has had certain learning experiences. The development of language is a good example. The child must be physically mature enough to move the muscles of his face and must be able to control his tongue well enough to make sounds correctly. He cannot, however, learn to talk if he does not hear others speak.

Cognitive Development

Cognitive processes are those which involve thinking, or intellectual activities which help the child solve problems and store information. Piaget, a well known developmental theorist, was one of the first to observe the many changes which occur in the child's cognitive abilities. He discovered that children are not just little adults, their cognitive ability in infancy is quite limited, their movements are mostly reflexive. As the child matures, he begins to develop better ways of organizing his thought processes so that finally he can think in very abstract terms. In the following paragraph we will describe some of the interesting observations which Piaget and other developmental theorists have made when they studied cognitive development.

As the infant matures he begins to explore his body and nearby objects. He will gaze intently at various objects and can recognize familiar ones. Yet when an object is hidden from his view under a blanket he will act as though the object no longer exists. A few months later he will search for the object, and appears to understand that objects are permanent. The infant's goal directed behavior also increases as his cognitive ability develops, he learns that certain responses will result in desired consequences. He learns that his cries will bring mother's comfort or that his grasping of a stuffed bear will cause it to squeak. During the next few years the child learns how to sort and

Developmental psychologists have tended to look at the child as progressing through various stages of development (see box) and most agree that there are certain developmental tasks which usually determine the beginning and end of these stages. These stages include physical (motor) development, cognitive development, and socialization (concern for others) of the child. Unless the appearance of signs of development are greatly behind schedule you should not become unduly concerned since these are only average estimates of when the child will develop new skills:

birth to 6 mos
    chest up
    reaches
    sits up with help
    sits on lap
    generalized excitement

6 mos to 1 yr
    sits in high chair
    grasps dangling objects
    pulls self up
    fear of strangers
    separation anxiety
    affection

1 yr to 2 yrs
    climbs
    stands alone
    walks
    some words
    shame
    jealousy

2 yrs to 3 yrs
    runs without falling
    arranges blocks in rows and towers
    turns pages 1 at a time in book
    kicks ball
    follows simple directions
    uses 2 word sentences
    disappearance of separation anxiety
    greater dependency on adults

3 yrs to 4 yrs
    hops with both feet
    rides tricycle
    colors with crayons
    imitation of others increases
    beginnings of abstract concept formation

4 yrs to 5 yrs
    throws ball overhead with some direction
    simple puzzles
    cuts simple lines with scissors
    has self awareness
    can learn to walk from school to home
    ethnic and racial awareness

5 yrs to 6 yrs
    skips alternating feet
    bounces and catches ball
    works more complex puzzles
    colors with some ability
    ability to selectively attend increases
    has concepts for most frequently encountered events
    moral standards and conscience

Figure 7. Examples of child development from birth to 12 years.

Figure 7 — *Continued.*

6 yrs to 7 yrs
  may ride bicycle
  jumps 12 inches
  may refuse to think about
  problem when he does not
  understand
  recall can improve if material is
  presented in meaningful clusters
  more fears develop
  feelings of guilt

7 yrs to 8 yrs
  may jump rope
  catches ball with one hand
  increases the complexity of
  words he can recall
  can arrange different length
  sticks in different rows
  prefers same sex as playmates

8 yrs to 9 yrs
  becomes more skilled in
  performance of physical
  activities
  jumps rope

classify new objects. He understands that cars have doors and horns and that you ride inside them, but he may refer to every car he sees as Mommy's car. He may say that all the round blocks should go together except for the small one because it will fit inside the largest of the squares so it should go with the squares. He tends to focus on only one aspect of a problem and so he will often make mistakes. For example, he may have noticed that all dogs have four legs so that when he first sees a sheep it too is labeled a doggy. Similarly, if his parents tend to argue over what to do when he misbehaves, he may blame himself rather than understanding that they have other problems which make them edgy.

The preschool child operates on what he intuitively believes to be true. During his elementary school years he will begin to use logical rules to solve problems. His thought processes will become more competent and flexible. He will begin to lose his rather self-centered perspective that everyone sees things from his point of view. As he becomes an adolescent he will begin to think more abstractly. He forms hypotheses and tests solutions to problems he encounters.

The Development of Moral Thought

Morals are a set of beliefs which help the individual determine what is right or wrong. The child's ability to reason in a moral way is related to his ability to empathize (understand the feelings or plight of others) and his level of cognitive development. To evidence good moral reasoning he must be able to focus on many aspects of the problem and understand what the consequence may be for each behavioral choice. The caretaker's task is to help the child learn to empathize and consider the consequences of his actions. Patience is required as this ability appears to develop slowly and may fluctuate a good deal depending on the type of situation.

Unfortunately the problem with the development of moral thought is that it doesn't correlate well with moral behavior. What people say they will do and what they will actually do are often two very different things (Kurtines and Greif, 1974). So even if the child has been exposed to a good deal of religious or other information about what is "right" and "wrong" he may behave in a contrary manner.

Recent research indicates that moral behavior is learned in much the same way as other behavior. How much moral behavior the child exhibits is determined by the moral behavior of admired models and the consequence of the child's moral reasoning. Caretakers must model what they teach and positively reinforce each appropriate moral behavior.

Self-Control and Delayed Gratification

For the very young child, resisting the temptation of an open dish of his favorite candy is extremely difficult, if not impossible. (He is better able to resist if someone is there who may punish him, but when he is left alone he will often give in to his desire.) He has not learned how to have self control, that is, he has not learned how to restrain his impulses. The child gradually learns self control in the same ways in which he acquires most of his new behaviors. He will learn through available models and the consequences of his actions.

In studies of children's ability to use self control, it has been found that some children have learned certain techniques to prevent themselves from yielding to temptation. Two of the more effective ones children typically employ are self-distraction and "not thinking" about the tempting situation (Mischel and Elbesen, 1970). Children with good self control will often distract themselves by playing games or looking away. Some try not to think about the tempting situation or use their imagination to make it seem less desirable.

The development of good self control as a child will enable the individual to delay gratification as an adult, thus making it possible for him to do things like going to college rather than getting married right after high school. The parent can help teach the child to have self-control and delayed gratification. Positive reinforcement by the caretaker for successful resistance of temptation will help the child learn to use positive statements as self-reinforcers when the caretaker is not there. Similarly the parent can teach the child by helping him to become distracted from temptation with something like a toy or game. It has also been found that coaching a child to say self controlling statements like "I must avoid the glass vase" will improve his ability to control himself (Hartig and Kanfer, 1973).

Several other factors will influence the child's ability to delay gratification. One of these is the expectation the child holds about the likelihood that he will receive the promised reward. If his parents have been inconsistent in their ability to follow through the child is not likely to learn delayed gratification. Also, if the child is only exposed to models who are impulsive he will have difficulty delaying gratification. In fact, even children with good self-control may lose control when they are around others who are impulsive. So, little Ginny, who always does her homework and never eats sweets, may lose control if she goes to spend the night with a friend who sits all evening in front of the TV with a box of candy.

Self control or "will power," as it is commonly known is an important skill. It is often the difference between a successful and competent individual and one who falls into "hopelessness" and "helplessness."

Social Development

Early affectionate attention from caretakers provides an important basis for social relationships. The young infant quickly comes to recognize his caretakers and will often fuss if they are not available. *Stranger anxiety* will appear in some children between the ages of six months and sixteen months (Schaffer and Emerson, 1964). Other children will not be fearful of strangers unless the stranger behaves oddly. It is possible that the appearance of stranger anxiety occurs because of painful sessions with the doctor or because he has learned that the appearance of a stranger means that Mother will be going out.

As the baby begins to move about, he uses his mother as a "safe base of operation" and may exhibit *separation anxiety* when Mother leaves him in an unfamiliar setting. This separation reaction usually peaks at two years of age and then diminishes. Infants will, however, vary in their reactions to the return of Mother. Recent research on infants' reactions have suggested that babies who get sufficient attention will give Mother a warm reception when she returns. Infants whose mothers are only attentive when they are in the mood are likely to cling at first to Mother upon her return and then squirm to get free. Mothers who seem insensitive to their baby's needs are likely to be avoided by their babies upon their return. These studies have not as yet shown that it is the mother's responsiveness causing the baby's response. It may be that the babies had different personalities to begin with, thus mothers would react differently to their baby's natures.

The preschool child spends most of his day in play. Though the child's play may look like a waste of time, it actually serves many constructive developmental purposes. Play can help the child deal with painful emotions and achieve conflict resolution (Erickson, 1963). It can be a way for the child to solve problems (Bruner, 1966) and it is an important means of learning about his environment (Piaget, 1963).

Through play the child develops a sense of mastery and competence. He regards his creative drawings and constructions as having great importance. The caretaker should encourage and praise the childs efforts. Playtime is a fun time and not a time for criticism or put downs. Caretaker comments like, "How stupid, cows can't fly" or "All you are doing is wasting paper and paint" are destructive. When a child is often criticized for his efforts his self-image and self-confidence suffer and in later life the child may be hesitant to attempt anything challenging or creative.

As the child comes in contact with other children he learns how to build friendships. The very young child only engages in parallel play, that is, he will be near other children but each is doing something different and interaction is minimal. As he nears school age he begins to engage in games and sharing activities. In elementary school peer influence is strong and the child usually prefers to play with children of his sex. By high school peer influence is generally stronger than that exerted by the parents. The parents' role is, however, one of increasing the child's independence and insuring that he has developed social skills.

Sex-Role Development

During the first year of life the infant does not think of itself as male or female. It only comes to call itself and act as male or female after it has been taught to do so by its caretakers. How well children adjust to their role of either male or female in this culture depends on the kinds of models to which they are exposed and the kind of reinforcement which they receive. Children, in this culture, are taught to model gender related behaviors from models of their own sex. Little boys learn to be like Daddy by watching what Daddy does, while little girls will imitate their mothers and other admired female models.

Affection for the model is important. For example, it is known that fathers who hug and act warmly toward their sons tend to have sons who are more masculine than those whose fathers are cool and aloof. Children who do not have a parent of the same sex from which they can model will still develop an appropriate sexual identity since the environment will generally provide other models of his sex. Little boys without a father, will often model after admired coaches or uncles.

Children need to feel good about being a part of their gender group. Certain stereotypes in our society, which parents sometimes impart upon their children, can cause the child to be confused or conflicted about his sexual identity. The young boy, whose mother always talks of men as being "dirty," "sinful," or as "always trying to take advantage of women," may feel very anxious about the possibility of becoming a man someday. Similarly, the young girl who has always heard her father make reference to women as "empty headed broads" may come to think poorly of herself since she too is a female.

Sexual Awareness

At first, the infant derives pleasure from touching and sucking. All objects, parts of his and other people's bodies will stimulate his curiosity. In the second year, he becomes fascinated with urine and feces. To him, they are not dirty, they are things to enjoy. Awareness of the difference between little boys' and girls' bodies often occurs by the 3rd or 4th year. Sex play with other children may also begin about this time and quite a few children begin to masturbate around this age, though they generally don't have orgasms. Recently, however, researchers have discovered that even some little infants can masturbate to orgasm. These are normal developmental behaviors and unless they are extremely frequent there is no reason to be alarmed.

The preschool child will also become aware and curious of the intimate relationship between his mother and father. It is not unusual for the child to be jealous of the parent of the same sex, and want to marry the other parent. Along with this can come a desire to sleep in the same bed with the parents or possible attempts to touch in sexual ways as well as acceptable affectionate ways. Sleeping all night in the parents' bed and sexual advances should be discouraged in a calm but firm manner. The child must come to realize that his parents' relationship is to be respected and that one day it will be fine for him to have such an intimate relationship with someone of the opposite sex. This problem and also excessive masturbation, can often be diminished if the child receives adequate affection such as caresses and kisses from *both* parents.

The child's increasing sexual curiosity and behavior is often a source of conflict and anxiety for parents who are unsure of what their response should be. In general, it is important that the child feel good about his body and its functions. If the child is made to feel that his body or genitals are dirty and untouchable, his guilt and self consciousness is likely to inhibit his later social interaction. In extreme cases, we see children who won't go to gym class or the swimming pool because they don't want others to see their body. In later life, these individuals often have marital problems because they can't enjoy sexual relations with their spouse, they still feel that those areas are dirty and untouchable.

Caretakers, however, can't let the child act without any restraint because our culture doesn't condone such behaviors as the child's masturbating during art class or his peeking in the girls' bathroom at school. Often the best approach is to teach the child that, while his body and its functions are to be appreciated, activities related to these areas are to be done in privacy and in some cases these activities should be enjoyed only when he is older. Training the child to be discreet will protect him from embarrassing and guilt inducing punishment from other adults who could observe the child appreciating his body. If you, yourself, don't feel you can approach such problems in a calm or appropriate manner a school counselor or relative who is comfortable with this area of development should be sought to help guide the child.

Chapter 7

Language, Intelligence, and Creativity

Communication

The new infant communicates with his environment with noises and loud wails. As its senses become better developed the infant associates the soft, friendly voices of people with the primary reinforcers which they provide. The human voice then becomes a welcome sound to the infant and serves as a secondary reinforcer. The infant soon begins to babble and wail to obtain the attention of others.

Research has shown that the more the infant is talked to, the more babbling will occur. Such babbling is the beginning of speech. Infants utter all sounds which make up human language, even those found in foreign languages. The infant, however, develops the speech patterns of its own culture through selective reinforcement and imitation.

Selective Reinforcement

The child's babblings and wailings are not very effective ways of communicating. The cold infant may cry out only to have a bottle of milk stuck in its mouth. Satisfying the baby is thus somewhat of a guessing game for the caretaker during the first two years.

Gradually, after specific words have been paired many times with reinforcement, the child learns to use words to make some of its wishes known. The child then hears a word like "mama" many times and begins to associate it with her presence and the reinforcement she brings. The child is soon reinforced for saying the word. It is a powerful word which brings help and soon other powerful words like hot, hungry, and daddy are learned.

At first, the child knows only a few words and is likely to use them indiscriminately. Upon first seeing a horse, it is not unlikely that the young child will call it a dog. These generalized responses are usually corrected by others and so the child increases its vocabulary to include the word "horse." Simple sentences appear around 30 months of age and become complete sentences around three years of age.

Since many professionals believe that children who are verbal at an early age are likely to become bright individuals, helping the young child learn to communicate is an important task. A simple reinforcement procedure, which requires that the child try to ask for what is wanted before it is given, should hasten learning. For example, if the infant reaches out for a cookie, the mother should prompt, "say cookie" and then patiently wait for the child to try the word before giving the cookie. Later the mother can encourage him to make a complete sentence.

Imitation

The above procedure of selective reinforcement works well, but if all the words we use had to be learned this way it would take us much longer to master the English language. Fortunately, the child learns to imitate the speech of others. Learning can occur simply by listening to those around him.

Questions

By the age of four, most children talk quite well and begin asking many questions. This behavior can be very irritating, but it is through this questioning process that the child learns about the world. Parents can help their children acquire knowledge by answering their questions accurately and in a simple, easy to understand manner. Stories and analogies are often very easy ways of explaining difficult subject matter to the child. For example: Billy was angry because his teacher made him stay in for throwing rocks. His mother asked Billy what he would do if he made his living as a teacher and he wanted to keep children from getting hurt. Fables like the "Little Boy Who Cried Wolf" are effective with most small children.

Sometimes caretakers make the mistake of laughing or getting mad at the child when he asks questions. Such reactions may punish curiosity. If the child is often discouraged from asking questions, he may not do well in school. In some cases he may make up his own answers when he is faced with puzzling situations. Case example: Jimmy asked his father why people can't fly. His father just laughed and laughed. The next day Jimmy got up on the roof and jumped off with his paper kite thinking it would make him fly.

Sometimes children's questions do become silly or excessive. A firm "that's enough questions right now" should get results if the parent then refuses to answer any more questions.

Words: The Meaning and Power of Words

The meaning which we ascribe to words is dependent on their context and our own personal experience with them as well as the definition given in the dictionary. Words obtain much of their meaning and evoke feelings through their association with consequences. The word "hot," for example, may recall a painful experience or consequence and the child may anxiously avoid any object which has previously been labeled "hot." The child who has thrown up after eating jelly beans may again feel a little sick when someone mentions the words.

Words which have sexual connotations acquire their social taboo from the consequences which parents and others place on them. Children are often punished for saying such words and told that they are dirty. These consequences may cause the child to feel anxious about these words and related sexual behaviors. Labeling sexual words as dirty may have later side effects. Some individuals never get over the idea that sexual things are unclean and so they may feel anxious with their marriage partner.

Another side effect of making sexual words taboo results when the child learns that these words get a lot of attention from friends and others. This consequence serves only to reinforce the child's behavior. Perhaps the best approach to discourage the use of inappropriate words by the child is to place mild consequences on this behavior. The parent can explain that such language offends some people and that it would be best if the child didn't use it. A few minutes in his room might be an adequate consequence if the child continues to use them.

Along with meaning, words acquire control over our behavior. This control, like meaning, is dependent on the context and the consequences with which it has been associated. The word "no" said in the context of the home may have a powerful effect over the child who has always been punished for disobeying. That same word, said to the child at school, by a teacher who rarely backs it up, is likely to have little effect. Similarly, when a mother says, "don't touch the wall plug, it will shock you," and the child touches it without getting shocked, he begins to learn that Mother is just a worrier and her cautions are not reliable. Parents should strive to give specific cautions that will give reliable guides to the child.

As you can see from the above discussion, the meaning of words and the control which they have over our behavior is not fixed as are dictionary definitions. Words have different meanings and effects on us depending on their context and our own individual experiences with them. Since words don't mean the same thing to everyone, there is room for misunderstanding. Communication between parents and their children can be improved if we take the time to make our meaning clear and check to see that we really understand what others have said to us.

Intelligence and Language

Language is of basic importance to man's intelligence. The possession of exceptional imitative skills and an ability to produce a wide range of sounds allow man to pass on valuable information from generation to generation. The parent is the primary source of information during the child's first six years of life. Professionals believe that during these early years more than three-fourths of the child's intellectual capacity is developed. It is important, then, that parents provide a stimulating environment in which the child can develop this capacity. This environment is best when it provides many varied experiences. Mobiles and interesting toys should always be available to the infant. Puzzles, games, and outings to such places as the park or zoo provide valuable experiences. Don't hesitate to try to explain things to the young child because he might not understand. Such explanations will reinforce his curiosity and stretch his capacity to comprehend.

Thinking: A Covert Language

Thinking, like talking, is behavior. Thinking seems to be a covert language which guides the person. Most psychologists believe that thinking and language develop about the same time. At first the child appears to do most of his thinking out loud. This seems to help him control his behavior. He may be heard saying things like "I play," "I go fast," or "Don't touch" to himself. By age 3 or 4, he begins to whisper to himself instead of talking out loud.

Rules

About age 3 or 4, children apparently begin to use language to develop rules. These rules help them to control their behavior in both new and old situations. As the child grows older, his rules become increasingly complex:

Ages 3 or 4: No go in street.
No jump on furniture.
Ages 6 or 7: I won't talk in class.
I don't ride with strangers.
Ages 8 or 9: Circles are round, Squares are like boxes, and Triangles have three sides.

Some of the rules children form may not be helpful:

I never clean up things. That's Mother's and the maid's job.
If I beg long enough, Mom always gives in.

Young children, like adults, can't always state the rules they go by, but we can sometimes infer their rules by observing what they do.

The child doesn't always form rules correctly:

duck—ducks—goose—gooses
walk—walked—run—runed.

Verbal Rules can make learning easier. The child who is learning to tie shoes may recite the rules he has learned in the following manner:

I put left one under right one and pull. Then I make a loop and wrap right one around and pull its loop through.

The parent can help the child learn new tasks quicker by teaching him to use rules:

1. Repeat each rule in the same way many times.
2. Ask the child to say what he is doing as he trys the task.
3. Make the task as simple as possible.
   a. Break it down into simple parts
   b. Make discrimination easy:
      ex: Dye one half of a shoestring green so that the child can easily tell the two strings apart as he first learns to tie his shoes.

Intelligence

What is intelligence? We can't observe it directly but we know that it involves the firing of neurons. Like the computer, the brain processes incoming information, transforms it, and sends messages back into the environment. While the brain is more forgetful than a computer, it is far more flexible. For example: When a computer receives a stack of information with one word misspelled, it will not process the information, and sends it back with an insulting message and some gibberish which seems like cursing (.'*???*38*). The human brain reads misspelled words and understands even mispronounced words with little problem. It is infinitely more flexible. It is also more creative in that it may respond differently to the same input while the computer's responses are always the same, given the same input.

Intelligence involves the brain's ability to process information and come up with adaptive responses. Or more simply, intelligence involves the learning process and our ability to perform. Like intelligence, learning can't be seen as it occurs. The only way that we can tell that learning has occurred or that a person is intelligent is by *observing* his performance. So what is important is how the person performs i.e.; what they do.

Many intelligence tests have been developed by psychologists in an attempt to estimate a person's ability to learn. There are many problems with these tests. They tend to be somewhat culturally biased and they are affected by a person's educational background. This means that some of the questions asked will be unfamiliar to the child. The child living in the inner city may not know what a cow is and so may call this animal a dog when asked to respond to its picture. This doesn't say anything about how fast or how well he can learn about cows.

With these limitations in mind, I.Q. scores assist teachers by allowing them to compare children to a standard, thus giving them an estimate of the child's ability in relation to other children of the same age. Normal intelligence scores range from around 85 to 115, with the mean I.Q. being 100. Most people (68% of the population) score in this range. More extreme scores indicate superior ability (above 115) or limited mental ability (below 85).

Scores are not fixed for life; they may vary depending on the child's experiences. By exposing the child to many educational experiences and encouraging his curiosity, it is likely that your child's I.Q. will increase. While heredity may influence our ability to perform intellectually, the environment is largely responsible for putting this genetic potential to work. Generally, a child's intellectual potential far exceeds that which is required in today's schools.

Creativity

Creativity is the human characteristic which brings novelty and change to our life. We all have this characteristic in varying degrees and we can all learn to be more creative. Without the ability to put elements together in new and unusual ways for new purposes we would be severely limited. There would be no wheel, no art, and no penicillin.

There is no really good way to tell which children are exceptionally creative. Some studies have indicated that these children are alone more than other children and may tend to be shy or withdrawn. They make good use of their time alone, engaging in fantasy, thought, and imaginative activities. These children do not feel pushed by their parents. They develop their individual interests at their own speed. The creative child isn't necessarily exceptionally intelligent, but is good at solving problems which require novel approaches.

The family of the creative child usually has respect for the child and encourages the child to develop his own beliefs. They trust his decision, and allow him freedom to explore his environment. They provide a varied and cultured environment for the child. Punishment is fair, predictable, and consistent, the child is encouraged to develop his own standards of right and wrong.

Learning To Be Creative

The creative child asks many imaginative questions. He wants to know "I wonder what would happen if," "how many different ways can," or "wouldn't it be neat if?" The wise parent will encourage him to seek realistic or original answers to these questions. Criticism of the child's choices should be minimal. The child's efforts should be praised whether or not he "colors within the lines" or chooses to copy the work of others. Copying is not necessarily bad. Through copying the skills of other creative individuals, the child can obtain basic skills which can later be blended into his own unique style. Lessons can also help the child develop basic skills. Formal training in basic skills is usually necessary because creative tendencies alone do not insure success. The child may have many ideas about how he would like his creations to turn out, but without basic techniques and skills he is likely to lack the ability to adequately demonstrate his creative ability. Case example: Peter is trying to draw his dream house. He has many novel ideas about this house. He has not, however, been taught how to make a drawing look three dimensional. He may become discouraged because he cannot make the house portray his thoughts. Choose an instructor with care! Lessons should be fun and not painful.

Fact and Fantasy

Sometimes children become very fanciful and imaginative. They tell such wild stories that parents often cannot determine if they are true. This is not unusual for very young children and should become less of a problem as the child matures. Young children's stories often come from TV or dreams. As the child grows, he begins to learn what is reality and what is fantasy. The child should be helped to make this distinction without severely punishing his creative imagination. The parent can help the child learn the difference between fantasy and reality by refusing to accept wild stories blindly and by consistently checking out his stories whenever it is possible. The child's storytelling can be corrected in the following ways:

Johnny: I saw a martian today. He had green pointed ears and purple eyes and he was eating a mars bar.
Mom: That sounds like you are telling me a story. Why don't you write a story about your monster.
Mom: Where have you been so late?
Baby: A big tiger chased me up a tree and I was too scared to come down.
Mom: I think you had best come in 10 minutes early tomorrow to make up for your being late today.
Child: Did you know that I can turn this water into gold?
Mom: I never have seen anyone do that, but people take mountain water which has little deposits of gold ore and sift out the gold.
Child: Watch me! (He fails)
Mother: Maybe if you go to college you'll be able to discover how to do something like that.

You can also help children understand the difference between reality and fantasy by frequently pointing out examples of each:

Mom: (reading a magazine) This is really an exciting true story.

Mom: (reading a story book) This author really has a good imagination!

Dad: (watching T.V.) Boy! didn't the make up artist know how to make that monster look scary.

Sometimes children tell wild stories because they are feeling insecure. In their stories, they brag about such things as magical powers or super abilities. These stories serve as a defense against threats to their security. The child who tells many such tales feels small, weak, unimportant, and insecure. He may be seen as lacking self confidence or trying to escape an unpleasant environment through fantasy.

Becoming Creative

The following are creative problem solving exercises. These exercises are fun and helpful in teaching creativity. They require flexible and novel approaches.

1. Write down all the uses you can think of for *one* brick (10 minutes). Example: use it as a hammer, put it under a flower pot.
2. Write down all the uses you can think of for a wooden box (10 minutes). Example: storage, table, bookshelf.

Breaking out of what psychologists call *set* is necessary to be creative. We tend to see things as having a set function and use. The creative person is able to imagine unusual and unexpected uses. Try to discover unique uses for conventional items around the house and test your own creativity.

Chapter 8

Adjustment Problems and Their Treatment

Spotting Problem Behaviors

Every child at times acts in ways that concern his parents. But how are we to decide which behaviors require correction? To answer this question we must again consider the following relationship:

$$\text{event} \longrightarrow \text{response} \longrightarrow \text{consequence}$$

Problem behavior can be recognized by its consequences. Problem behaviors have undesirable consequences for either the child or others. Undesirable consequences include those that may prevent happiness, self actualization, and survival. By considering the consequences (or those possible) it is much easier to decide which behaviors to correct and what rules to make.

Consider the following examples:

Example 1: Mrs. A. and Mrs. B. have become concerned about their sons. Each woman's son spends 6 hours a day drawing. Both boys are in seventh grade. The teachers tell Mrs. A that her son never takes notes, just draws and so he makes poor grades. After school he shuts himself in his room and draws. He seems unhappy and has no friends. Mrs. B's son makes good grades, even though he often draws in class. After school he draws the outlines for football banners so that other students can finish painting them. His marvelous skill has made him a school hero.

Example 2: Both Jerry and Pete are witty. They often make others laugh. Jerry's joke, however, often cuts others down and other children usually exclude him. Pete, on the other hand, never makes a joke at the expense of another child. He is always welcome.

Example 3: Both Marilyn and Jane's mothers encourage them to try out for cheerleader. Marilyn is lovely and athletically coordinated. She is well received as she tries out on stage. Jane is overweight and awkward. The student audience boos and jeers.

In the above examples, the behaviors are similar but the consequences are very different. As parents we must consider not only the behavior but also its consequences, and furthermore, we must teach the child to foresee the possible consequences of his actions.

In almost all important actions, there is an element of risk such as actual physical danger or loss of self esteem. Initially the parents decide what risk the child will take. We decide when the infant can be taken outside and what kind of toys he will have. Gradually, the child initiates more and more actions on his own. The child who has not been taught to foresee the consequences of his actions may continually make disastrous mistakes, while the child who has been excessively cautioned will be afraid to take a risk. We shall call the former child's behavior Type B and that of the latter, Type C behavior. We can add to these two categories Type A behavior, which is characteristic of the child who realistically considers the consequences and takes risks when such actions are most likely to result in positive and constructive consequences.

Characteristics: The Type A, B, and C Child

TYPE A THE ADJUSTED CHILD	(1) Is not afraid to make friends and express affection. (2) Rarely has accidents which result in physical harm to self or others. (3) Is active and has several good friends. (4) Likes to try new things as long as they aren't extremely risky. (5) Can delay gratification of immediate desires for long term gain rewards, but seldom has to because plans ahead.
TYPE B THE OVERLY BOLD CHILD	(1) Often injures self or others. (2) Often in trouble with neighbors or school personnel. (3) Fights with other children. (4) May tease animals or start fires. (5) Lies, cheats, or steals. (6) Doesn't plan ahead. (7) Does poorly in school. (8) Doesn't delay gratification, wants everything now. (9) Always gets angry and hostile when he can't get his way.

TYPE C THE OVERLY CONSERVA- TIVE CHILD	(1) Is afraid of change—everything must stay in the same place. (2) Won't take risks even when he is assured by parents that it is okay. (3) Stays by self and has almost no friends. (4) Becomes overly concerned about germs, sickness, or death. (5) Appears unhappy most of the time and cries easily. (6) Has many fears that other children don't. (7) Doesn't feel he deserves much—thinks others don't like him. (8) Sulks for long periods of time if criticized or things don't go right.

Most children do not, however, clearly exhibit A, B, or C behavior, they often fall in between these categories. And, too, sometimes children act very different from one situation to another. At Grandma's house many children resort to a number of Type A behaviors, while in a stranger's home, they often show more Type C behavior than is usual.

It must be remembered that infants and very young children are not capable of Type A behavior. This behavior is learned through effective child management. It does not "just come along with age."

Abnormal Behavior: A Definition

Just exactly what is meant by abnormal behavior? Even some professionals cannot agree but we all have our own idea and "know" what it is. In the authors' opinion abnormal behavior is behavior which results in undesirable consequences for that person or others. Of course, all of us may occasionally behave in ways that are not realistic or functional. We do, however, manage to take care of our affairs and usually feel satisfied with our lives. When dysfunctional or irrational behaviors begin to seriously impair the quality of one's life or that of others, then this behavior is abnormal.

Abnormal behavior, then, is often a matter of degree rather than kind. For example, all children are fearful to some degree. The child, however, who has no fear, as well as the child who has so many fears that he will not leave the house, is abnormal. Their behaviors will result in consequences that may seriously impair their lives.

The context in which the behavior occurs must also be considered. Children from northern inner cities areas often have trouble adjusting when they are moved to small southern towns because physical aggression is a frequent and accepted way of dealing with others in the first context. In a quiet, southern town this child may be labeled abnormal.

How Abnormal Behavior Comes About

There are many, many theories about the origin of abnormal behavior. The authors believe that most abnormality is the result of faulty learning and that no physical basis exists. The child, then, has learned to act immaturely and has failed to learn the functional coping skills which are necessary in a given situation.

Coping Skills

All children (and adults too) must deal with frustration. We become frustrated when obstacles encountered in our physical or social space block our goals. Personal frustration, which may be real or imagined, occurs due to some personal limitations. Conflict frustrations occur when we must choose between equally desirable goals or when a goal has negative and positive consequences associated with it.

The simplest kind of conflict frustration is called approach-approach. Here we must choose between two positive goals, such as deciding which shirt or dress to wear or whether to go to a movie or a play. We do not believe that anyone has ever developed any real problems from this type of conflict.

Conflict which involves two negative (or unpleasant) goals is called avoidance-avoidance. When this conflict is severe it can lead to attempts to get out of the situation. Cases of amnesia, going "crazy," and even suicide may reflect such an intense avoidance conflict. Sayings such as "out of the frying pan into the fire" and "caught between the devil and the deep blue sea" reflect this kind of conflict. The child that must choose between studying and getting poor grades is experiencing such a conflict.

The third type of conflict occurs when a single goal has both negative and positive aspects associated with it. This is quite common and we all experience such love/hate, want to/don't want to feelings at one time or another. This type of conflict is known as approach-avoidance. This kind of conflict causes us to vascillate in that as we get closer to the goal the negative features come into play and we retreat. As we retreat, the negative avoidance tendency decreases and the positive aspects cause us to again approach the goal. We may find ourselves going back and forth, back and forth.

The fourth and final type of conflict is really just a more complex form of the third one. In double approach-avoidance conflict, there are two goals each of which has both negative and positive features associated with it. Many real life examples may come to mind and we are sure that you can see how this results in a great deal of frustration for your child.

There are obviously successful and not so successful ways of dealing with the various forms of frustration. When the child is unsuccessful at resolving conflicts, abnormal behaviors may result and these can take many forms. The child may become aggressive and lash out, or moody, first happy, then sad, or become distant and uninterested in anything.

The Depressed Child

Sometimes a child may be labeled lazy, stupid or aloof when he is actually depressed. According to Seligman (1975), the depressed child is likely to have an intense feeling of hopelessness. His depression is usually triggered by a loss of face, privileges, or loved one. When children are depressed they tend to believe themselves to be worthless and to feel like there is nothing that they can do to change. When good things do happen they tend to diminish their significance and tend to deny their part in bringing them about.

Children's depression is a more prevalent and serious problem than professionals once thought. In one urban school system 25 to 30 percent of the children surveyed showed marked depression. Fifteen percent showed severe depression. For most children depression does not dissipate quickly, it is not just a stage. Most of the children surveyed were still depressed six months later.

Signs of Suicide

When a child is suicidal he will usually show marked changes in his daily habits. He may withdraw, become emotional, change the amount he eats, or lose interest in favorite things. His grades may drop and he may make negative comments about his worthlessness. He will generally view his situation as hopeless (Seligman, 1975). Other indicators are giving away prized possessions, saying "I won't be around then," or coming right out and threatening to kill himself.

If the caretaker suspects the child is suicidal, then the child should be confronted gently by the caretaker. The caretaker must listen carefully and be attentive as these children need reassurance and a sense of purpose. Such messages as, "I do count" and "I can change things so that they will be better" need to be conveyed to the child.

The following checklist may be helpful in spotting abnormal behaviors such as anxiety, stress, and depression which are not being successfully coped with.

Behavior exhibited by child.	Sometimes	Never
Wets bed (over age 5)		
Sets fires		
Lies		
Cruel to animals		
Uncooperative		
Doesn't play with other children		
Doesn't eat regularly		
Does not ask questions		
Steals		
Fights		
Argues		
Nightmares		

Take data on these behaviors for at least a week, preferably two, in order to get an accurate measurement of what behaviors the child consistently manifests. If the child scores in the "sometimes" category on the first three items then professional help is recommended. If the child scores in the "sometimes" category on the remaining items, you can try the procedures in this book for a few months before seeking help. The greater the number of items on which he scores in the "sometimes" category, the more likely it is that he needs professional help.

Problems That Aren't Problems

There are numerous problem behaviors that appear in many children at particular ages which should not be cause for alarm unless they are extreme in nature. Included in these are such nuisance behaviors like picky eating, telling whoppers, and refusal to comply with requests. If caretakers become overly concerned when such behaviors first occur, they risk overreacting in a way that will reinforce that behavior with negative attention or create a power struggle. To discourage these behaviors try reinforcing an incompatible behavior or ignoring the behavior. If the behavior persists, discuss the problem with the child and then decide with him some mildly aversive consequence to discourage it. Discussion of the problem at hand is always important as in the following example:

At 5 years of age, Betty suddenly developed picky eating habits. She would eat only green beans and baked chicken. Her mother began to nag her, took her to the doctor, and even tried to force her to eat by pushing the food into her mouth. Betty's problem worsened. She could hold a mouthful of food for as long as 30 minutes without swallowing. During therapy, discussion with Betty revealed that she had become afraid that she would be fat and that certain foods would cause her to break out in bumps. She was really afraid to eat. Furthermore, the pressure her mother put on her made her feel anxious and nauseous so that she really didn't feel hungry. In exploring her mother's reasons for pushing her to eat, it evolved that she felt that having a skinny child, who didn't eat right, made her look like a bad mother to others. Also, she felt the child's resistance was a sign that she hated her mother. Such unfortunate misunderstanding and power struggles can ruin the relationship between a parent and child.

Helping and being nice are not always beneficial. Consider the following:

SITUATION	CONSEQUENCE OF HELPING OR BEING NICE	ALTERNATIVE
The Super Mom who does everything for her daughter.	Daughter doesn't learn to take responsibility or work toward a goal.	Positively reinforce daughter for doing for herself and finding her own solutions.
A child who always criticizes and gossips about others is reassured by mother that she is liked when she isn't.	She continues to annoy others and remains friendless.	Help her by telling her the truth so she can do something to change.
Mother who never thinks of herself. She never takes time for herself and refuses any help.	She feels bitter toward her "ungrateful" family and takes it out on them in subtle passive aggressive ways. Family feels guilty because she works too hard and resents her unsolicited help.	Takes time and money for herself. Demands respect and consideration from family. She feels good and has more to give of herself.

SITUATION	CONSEQUENCE OF HELPING OR BEING NICE	ALTERNATIVE
Woman tells her child she will help with a social function, knowing she won't have time.	She does a poor job, the social function flops and the child is angry and the mother feels guilty.	Tell the child not to count on her, but she will do what she can when she does have time.

Now consider the following examples of appropriate ways to help.

(1) Mother teaches child to care for self.
(2) Mother helps out in real emergency.
(3) Praise for specific constructive achievements.
(4) Being emotionally sensitive and supportive.
(5) Mother models how to use a can opener, but allows the child to do it for herself.

How Do You Find Professional Counseling for the Child?

A child psychologist may be located through a number of sources. Most large cities have mental health facilities that employ psychologists. The counselors at most schools have access to psychologists for referral purposes. Either the local or state psychological association can usually provide the names of qualified psychologists upon request. Most states now have a state licensing board which keeps a roster of psychologists licensed to practice in that state. The psychology department at a nearby college or university should also prove to be a helpful source of information. Finally, other professionals such as attorneys, doctors, ministers, and dentists usually know of psychologists with whom they have personally worked and to whom they can refer you.

Other trained professionals include child psychiatrists, social workers, marriage and family counselors, and ministers. Most states have some sort of regulatory board covering psychologists, psychiatrists, and social workers. Nonregulatory certification boards usually exist for marriage and family counselors, ministers, and hypnotherapists. These agencies can supply the names of competent and ethical professionals.

What Kinds of Treatment Might Be Expected?

Numerous therapeutic methods are available. It is difficult to suggest what might be appropriate without knowledge of the individual involved. The child psychologist should be able to tell you what he feels is most appropriate. If after a period of time you do not agree, you should discuss your feelings with the psychologist. If the discussion is unsatisfactory you should indicate that you want a second opinion. Your therapist should be able to refer you to another psychologist. Some forms of therapy seem to work well for one case and not so well for another. As the kids say, "Different strokes for different folks."

Some typical forms of therapy might include: family therapy, play therapy, contingency management, and hypnosis. The following are only a few examples of the many types of therapy available for children.

Family therapy typically involves the whole family. The child's problem is seen as evolving out of the familial relationship and should be treated in that context. Problems in communication among the family members are often the focus of therapy. Each member's fears and expectations are explored.

Play therapy allows the child an opportunity to act out any emotional feelings via toys since the disturbed child may not be able to use words to describe his problems. The professional can interpret the child's play and help him work through his emotional conflicts.

Contingency management involves arranging the reinforcers in the environment in such a way that they follow desired behavior. This may be as simple as giving a child a treat after doing his homework or as complex as attempting to shape up responsibility or trustworthiness behavior.

Hypnosis is a form of relaxation. During the hypnotic state desired suggestions for behavioral changes may be communicated to the child. These suggestions are more likely to be accepted in this state as opposed to a normal waking state. For deepseated problems hypnoanalysis may be indicated.

Not all psychologists use the techniques just described. You might ask the psychologist if he does use a particular technique if you feel that that is the treatment you desire. As mentioned earlier, the psychologist can refer you to someone who does have an expertise other than his own if the occasion should arise.

Chapter 9

More Principles of Child Management

In this chapter we will present a more technical explanation of how positive reinforcement can be used to teach and maintain desired behavioral responses. The technical material in brackets can be eliminated without impairing your understanding of this chapter. This chapter will answer questions such as, "How can I reinforce a behavior if it never occurs?" and "Do I have to reinforce the child every time he makes the desired response?" As you will see from our discussion in this chapter, once a behavior begins to occur, it can usually be maintained with only occasional positive reinforcement.

Shaping

When a child does not ever behave in the desired way, it may be that he doesn't want to or that he can't remember or that he doesn't know how to do what you have asked him to do. In any of the above cases, the desired behavior can be obtained through a technique called shaping. (Also called the method of successive approximations.) Shaping requires that you watch for small improvements or close approximations to the desired response and then immediately, positively reinforce that response. As the child's behavior improves you require a more perfect response. This is a gradual technique which prevents the child from failing and thereby eliminates much of the strain and frustration of learning a new response pattern.

When it is the case that the child doesn't behave in the desired way because he can't remember or doesn't want to change, positive reinforcement is given whenever the child does any portion of the desired response pattern. Therefore, if Pigpen's mother wants him to dress and wash himself better, she can positively reinforce such things as brushed hair or fresh clothes. So, in spite of the five days of dirt that has accumulated beneath his fingernails, Pigpen's mother might say "I am pleased with your combed hair and fresh shirt." Later when he has also cleaned his fingernails she might say "I'm going to take you to a movie since you look so handsome."

When the response pattern is so complex that the child hasn't yet learned to do it, shaping is the best method to use. If little Albert is learning to ride his new two wheel bike, he must first learn to balance properly. The teacher can hold the bike at first, gradually fading away the amount of time he supports the bike as Albert learns to balance for himself. The teacher is careful to observe when Albert is holding the handlebars in a straight and steady way so that he can reinforce this part of the response pattern. Academic skills are also best taught by shaping. The child must learn to count before he can understand that 10 is more than 5.

As you can see, shaping involves a little bit more each time before the behavior is reinforced again. If too much is required, though, the behavior may extinguish. If that happens use smaller steps until you get compliance and make sure that the reinforcer is appropriate. If the child is satiated (has had enough), the reinforcer will have lost its effectiveness, at least temporarily. This is *more* likely to happen with food or treats (primary reinforcers) than with attention or money rewards (secondary reinforcers).

Schedules of Reinforcement

Once a child has learned a response pattern, he may need to be motivated to continue behaving in this desired way. It is usually inefficient, undesirable, and not necessary to continue reinforcing every appropriate response. There are two methods to change from continuous reinforcement of a new behavior to a maintenance procedure or schedule of reinforcement for appropriate responses. The ratio method reinforces a block of responses rather than each and every response. The word ratio is used because these schedules of reinforcement are based on the rate at which a behavior occurs. The more often the response is made, the more often the child will be reinforced. There are two types of ratio schedules, fixed and variable ratio. The interval method involves reinforcing the appropriate response only after a certain amount of time has past. There are also two types of interval schedules, fixed and variable interval. In choosing the best way to schedule positive reinforcement you should consider the speed, duration, and frequency with which you would like the response to occur.

Fixed Ratio Schedules*

With a fixed ratio schedule of reinforcement you can tell the child that he will receive his reward after he has made a set number of correct responses. The child can be told that he may watch 30 minutes of television upon completion of 30 homework problems. Many video games work this way, the child must earn a certain number of points before he gets to enter his name on the best players list. Fixed ratio schedules generate a steady rate of responding. After each reward there is often a short rest or pause after which the rate is again steady. So Bobby may mow one yard and stop for a cold drink before tackling the next yard.

*The remainder of this chapter is technical and can be omitted without impairment of further reading.

Variable Ratio Schedules

To use a variable ratio schedule you must decide on the average number of times you think will maintain the rate of a desired behavior. If you decide that Bobby's newly acquired good manners should be praised on the average of every ten appropriate responses, you need to develop a schedule of reinforcement that varies around and averages out to every ten correct responses. That is, you might reinforce him with praise on the fifth correct response, then on the seventh, then the tenth one and then the fifteenth one, etc. Variable ratio schedules deliver positive reinforcement after a varying number of correct responses so that the child doesn't know when he will be reinforced. He soon learns however, that the more often he behaves correctly, the more attention (reinforcement) he will receive. Consequently, this schedule generates a high rate of responding without any pauses. Selling door to door and games of chance, like those in Las Vegas, deliver reinforcement on this schedule. With children, pop tests and surprise treats are examples of reinforcers which are delivered on a variable ratio schedule. This is a very efficient way to deliver reinforcement because the caretaker only occasionally has to attend to the child's appropriate response. This is a good schedule for teaching children to work by themselves for long periods of time. The caretakers need only occasionally seek out the child and praise whatever constructive project the child has started. This approach will ultimately give the caretaker much more free time than reinforcing a child who begs for help and attention.

Interval Schedules of Reinforcement

Sometimes it is easier to deliver reinforcement when the child has made the appropriate response within a particular segment of time. This is called an interval schedule of reinforcement because the passage of time determines the delivery of a reward rather than the rate at which the child works. As with ratio schedules, the interval before reinforcement is set for fixed interval schedules and it varies around an average time length for variable interval schedules.

Fixed Interval Schedules

To use a fixed interval schedule you must decide on a fixed amount of time in which the child must make at least one appropriate response in order to obtain his reward at the end of the interval. Usually the child will not do much during the first part of the interval, then he will work quickly to finish up before the deadline. So when a test is announced for next Friday (FI1) and he has a week to prepare, he will often put off studying until Thursday night and then cram to catch up. Similarly, if you tell your child that he has a week to clean up his room and mow the grass expect little to nothing during the first half of the week and much effort as the deadline approaches. Unfortunately, many parents do not realize that this kind of pattern is to be expected from a fixed interval schedule. And so they try to counter procrastinations through criticizing and nagging at the child to get busy and get the work done. A way to eliminate this slack period is to use a variable interval schedule or to find an immediate daily reinforcer for completion of a portion of the work.

Variable Interval Schedules

This last schedule that we are going to discuss produces a fairly rapid and steady rate of responding much like the fixed ratio schedule. Pauses are eliminated since the child cannot predict when the reinforcer will become available and he must constantly respond in order to maximize the probability of reinforcement. The passage of time is what determines the delivery of the reinforcement. The interval is not fixed, varying in length on some predetermined schedule that only the caretaker knows. For example, if the teacher announces that quizzes will be unannounced (ie pop tests) the child must constantly be prepared since he cannot predict when it will be given. To relate this to our example of getting the child to clean his room and mow the grass, you could tell him that you are going to spot check his progress each day and if any work has been done it will be recorded. When the week ends the overall job will be inspected and his allowance will be based on the amount completed, plus a bonus will be given if a certain amount of work was completed during each spot check.

As a whole, variable schedules are more resistant to extinction than fixed schedules. Many times caretakers inadvertently set up variable schedules that then maintain such things as temper tantrums, nagging, and incessant crying. One such example is when a parent decides that he will only occasionally respond to the child's begging for candy. So the child crys 5, then 10 minutes, and finally the parent gives in to the child so he doesn't have to listen to the child's begging anymore. This occasional reinforcement makes extinction much more difficult than if he had attended to the child's begging each and every time it occurred.

Discrimination

Discrimination refers to the way we learn to respond to the many complex stimuli that we encounter in our environment. We learn to respond appropriately to cues in our environment because they have been associated with various consequences. A cue for positive reinforcement is called a discriminative stimulus (S^D). A cue for extinction is called an esse delta (S^Δ).

A person smiles when we look him in the eye. We say hello and he says hello back. The smile is a cue (S^D) for a pleasant social interaction. A person frowns as you approach him. You say hello and he walks past you without speaking. The frown becomes a cue (S^Δ) for not speaking next time you meet someone who is frowning.

Generalization

This process is the reverse of discrimination. Here the child applies what he has learned about one situation or set of cues to other similar situations. Sometimes this process helps and other times it hinders his ability to learn new behaviors. So when little Albert learned how to pay at the cashier's lane at one store he will have little trouble understanding what he is to do in a new store. Similarly, once he has learned to add single column numbers, double numbers are learned much easier.

Sometimes generalization hinders the child because he over generalizes. Therefore, after seeing many horses, he may incorrectly call the zebra at the zoo a horse.

By and large, generalization is a useful learning process for the child as it allows him to respond to previously unexperienced stimuli. Education is based, to a large extent, on generalization.

Chapter 10

Ideas for Behavior Programs

In this chapter you will find some examples of programs for some common problems which caretakers face. These programs are included only to give you ideas for designing programs for your particular child or group of children. No one program will work for all situations. Designing effective programs requires intimate knowledge of the children and available resources as well as an adequate understanding of behavioral principles. For caretakers, just beginning such programs, consultation with a behavior therapist would be helpful.

Behavior programs will require some creative planning and extra planning on your part in the beginning, but the end result can be very rewarding. Ultimately they should save you time and grief as the child's behavior improves. These programs should not, however be initiated before other procedures like using more praise or logical consequences have been tried, since they often involve the use of material rewards which are not generally awarded by our culture for these behaviors. That is, when the child becomes an adult no one is going to give him extra TV time for keeping up with the latest information in his professional field. We have found, however, that children often learn how to use such incentives for self reinforcement after being involved in a successful behavior program. Such programs help teach self control and delayed gratification to children who have not learned this from their environment. For those children who already have learned a good deal of self control and who work because it is intrinsically reinforcing to them to do well, programs which use material rewards are not necessary and may even result in resentful reactions on their part. Such programs should only be initiated when the child's behavior cannot be controlled with less formal behavioral methods. These programs should be faded out as soon as the desired behavior has become well established.

The general procedure for designing a program is given below:

Step 1: *Specify* a goal behavior. Decide exactly what behavior you desire to see changed and what responses the child will emit when the program succeeds.

Step 2: *Observe* what activities are reinforcers for the child. These will be the things he prefers to spend his time doing and the places he asks to go.

Step 3: *Record* how often the child performs the behavior over the period of a week or two. We will call this period of time a *baseline* observation.

Step 4: *Decide* what you think might be a good reinforcer for this behavior, and then make obtaining this reinforcer contingent on the child's completion of a specified amount of behavior.

Step 5: Continuously *observe* and *record* how often the behavior is performed.

Step 6: *Follow through and be consistent.* Positively reinforce him if he completes the agreed amount of behavior.

Step 7: *Re-evaluate* your procedure often. If the child is failing to meet the criteria, several things may be wrong. What you may be asking may be too difficult or, more likely, the reinforcer is not really desirable.

You should not expect a program to automatically work forever. Many factors, such as reinforcers and satiation, schedules of reinforcement, past history of the child, etc., will influence the effectiveness of the program.

Case 1: Will not study

Step 1: Specify—Day Dreaming Annie's mother consults with her teacher and it is decided that Annie should sit at her desk for 30 minutes each day after school and read.

Step 2: Observe—Annie likes to play with Susie, next door, after school.

Step 3: Record—Annie is told to study for 30 minutes when she gets home. Mother makes random checks to see how long Annie is studying. Out of 3 checks per day during which Annie's studying behavior was timed for a total of 9 minutes she was only averaging 3 minutes after one week of baseline data taking.

Step 4: Decide—Annie's mother decides that Annie will be allowed to go to Susie's if she is sitting at her desk reading for at least 8 minutes out of the 9 minutes of random time sampling her mother conducts each day during the study period. She explains the new program to Annie and takes Annie's reaction into consideration.

Step 5: Observe and Record—Annie's mother collects data on the amount of time she spends studying now, using the same method she did to obtain the baseline.

Step 6: Consequence—Annie is only allowed to go outside and play if she has studied long enough.

Step 7: Re-evaluate—If Annie is studying better and often getting to go out to play afterward, then the program is working. If not, the program needs to be modified so that the child receives some reinforcement for engaging in studying behavior. Once the child begins to be reinforced by better grades, the program can be discontinued because she will study on her own.

Case 2: Failing in math

Step 1: Specify—Billy's mother and math teacher decide he should do at least 30 math problems each day for homework.

Step 2: Observe—Mother observes that Billy watches more than 2 hours of TV each day after school.

Step 3: Record—She records the number of math problems Billy will complete each day after school.

Step 4: Decide—Since watching TV is likely to be a good reinforcer for Billy, the ratio between studying and watching television can be four to one; that is, 30 math problems will result in two hours of TV watching.

Step 5: Observe and Record—Does Billy correctly work thirty math problems after school? Mother records the exact number.

Step 6: Consequence—Mother makes certain that the four to one ratio between work and play is adhered to. She can also allow Billy to engage in reinforcing activities other than TV watching, if this works better.

Step 7: Re-evaluate—Mother looks at how many problems he is working. If the program is working he should be doing at least 30 problems a day and his math scores on tests should be improving.

Case 3: Fear of reading out loud in reading group

Step 1: Specify—Timmy is to read in a loud voice when he is called upon.

Step 2: Observe—Timmy responds well to praise.

Step 3: Record—Timmy does not read when he is called upon, he only hangs his head and blushes.

Step 4: Decide—Timmy recites out loud from some book alone and then reads for parents who praise his accomplishment, then he reads for teacher alone, who also praises his accomplishment. Recordings of his voice are made then played back by his parents, who praise his competent performance. He reads with other students in small groups the size of which is gradually increased until the entire class participates.

Step 5: Observe and Record—Timmy's teacher records the number of times the child reads when he is called upon and the number of times he refuses.

Step 6: Consequence—Immediate reinforcement in the form of praise for performance follows his reading out loud.

Step 7: Re-evaluate—Timmy should be reading out loud each time, if not some consequence such as going to the zoo at the end of each successful week might be added.

Case 4: Acceptance and cooperation with other children

Step 1: Specify—Shy Sally should be playing with the other children at least 50% of the time on Saturday and Sunday.

Step 2: Observe—All of the children respond well to praise or treats.

Step 3: Record—Sally's mother records the amount of time she is included in the activities of other children by observing ten minutes out of two hours in the morning and then ten minutes out of two hours in the afternoon. She records the amount of time Sally is engaged in the desired behavior.

Step 4: Decide—All of the children are reinforced with treats and social reinforcement when Sally is included in their play. They are praised with social reinforcement, such as "I am glad to see that all of you children are having such a good time playing together." This can be done on a random basis, once in the morning and once in the afternoon, at varying times when Sally has been included during that time sampling interval.

Step 5: Observe and Record—Using a time sample of ten minutes out of two hours in the morning and ten minutes out of two hours in the afternoon, Sally's mother records the amount of time she is now playing with other children.

Step 6: Consequence—She reinforces the children with treats and praise if they have included Sally. The children are not told, however, that the treats are contingent on Sally's being included. Reinforcement will work even when the children don't realize that they are being reinforced.

Step 7: Re-evaluate—If the behavior record indicates that Sally is not being included any more often than she was during the baseline then a new approach may be necessary. Perhaps Sally will have to be reinforced directly for playing with other children.

Case 5: Achievement

Parents should not be over-zealous in their attempt to push for high achievement. The child who is accepted by other children and making acceptable academic progress, can be encouraged to do well in school through positive reinforcement procedures, but he should not be pushed beyond his capabilities. A program similar to the one discussed under Failure in Math could be used.

Case 6: Aggression

Step 1: Specify—Aggressive Andy must learn to get along without shouting at and physically harming other children.

Step 2: Observe—Andy likes to spend time building models.

Step 3: Record—The frequency of aggressive responses are tabulated on a daily basis and kept on a chalk board in the kitchen.

Step 4: Decide—A good reinforcer for Andy has been building models. His father tells him that if his rate of aggression is fifty percent below baseline at the end of the week, he will buy him a model of his choice in a certain price range. If aggressive responses occur above this criteria during the week, he will lose the model, and each aggressive response will be followed by 15 minutes of time out. Time out will be conducted in a room which is devoid of reinforcers, such as toys and television. At the end of the time out period, he will be readmitted to the play environment and no mention of the time out will be made. Social reinforcement will be given as soon as the child engages in a cooperative play/non-aggressive play activity.

Step 5: Observe and Record—Data is collected to determine if Andy's aggression is at least fifty percent below baseline.

Step 6: Consequence—Andy should be receiving a model at the end of at least two weeks. If not, either this was not sufficiently reinforcing to maintain the response, or the goal for Andy was too high. The program needs to be reassessed.

Step 7: Re-evaluate—If Andy is doing much better, a more stringent criteria can be required. He may now be asked to further decrease his aggressive behavior before receiving a new model.

Case 7: Toilet Training

This is an area of concern for a number of parents. A simple, but effective method developed by Azrin and Foxx (1974) can be applied when the child is physiologically able to control the sphinctor muscles of the bladder. This control usually occurs between 2 and 3 years of age. The caretaker should not use harsh, punishing methods. It is best to take a block of time, such as 4 or more hours. During this time have the child drink a large quantity of liquids, such as juices, so that the frequency of urination is increased, thus giving you plenty of opportunities to administer positive reinforcement. To facilitate this procedure use a doll that can be made to drink and "wet" as a model. Play with the child and have him give the doll a drink and watch the doll urinate. Indicate to the child that it would be nicer if the doll would use the potty chair. Then have the child drink the juice and encourage him to use the potty chair. If he does use the potty chair, reinforce the child with praise and other reinforcers like sodas or potato chips. Periodically check to see if the pants are dry. Praise and give more reinforcers and juice, etc. if the child hasn't wet his pants. If the child's pants are wet, instruct him to change them and withhold reinforcement until the child actually wets in the potty chair.

Case 8: Nailbiting

Nailbiting and Cuticlebiting is the name of a little book on self control procedures written by Dan and Fredda Perkins (1976). Their program involves increasing awareness by spending 10 minutes each morning slowly bringing your hands to your mouth saying this is what I am not going to do anymore. They also recommend that you keep track of how often you bite your nails during the day by marking a 3x5 notecard, later graphing each day's data. Other suggestions include rewarding and punishing yourself as well as engaging in competing activities, such as keeping ones hands folded. Finally, contracting is discussed and examples are included.

Fading Out Program

When caretakers first learn about behavioral programs, they often wonder how long they will have to use this approach and what kind of effects it will have on the child. This is a legitimate concern as taking data can be time consuming. Ideally, children should all do what is "right" and "good" because they are supposed to. Unfortunately, this is not the case. A child is socialized through internalizing the values and standards of his parents and peers. This process may seem to occur "naturally." But if the situation is analyzed certain behavioral processes are shaping the child's behavior. When we find it necessary to place a child on a program we are merely attempting to apply these behavioral principles more consistently and effectively. As the desired behavior begins to occur it should provide intrinsic reinforcement thus it often becomes self maintaining. Also, reinforcement from parents, peers, and significant others helps to maintain behavior. The more numerous sources and types of reinforcement you pair with the desired response the better established that response pattern will become.

A facetious example might help clarify this point. Junior had trouble doing his work in school because he was too busy being the class clown. His teacher astutely realized that the powerful reinforcer of peer attention was much more desired by Junior than doing his math problems. She decided to reward Junior with an M&M each time he was on-task. After a while he would work only if given an M&M. Now he can be seen walking down the school hallway carrying a large sack of M&M's and his dentist's bill is astronomical.

Junior's teacher's mistake was to only use a primary reinforcer. A much better approach would have been to pair praise (social reinforcement) with the M&M's and gradually fade the M&M's out, replacing them with appropriate reinforcers such as attention for work completed and free time upon successful task completion. Perhaps Junior will never become a mathematician, but he can be brought to the point that appropriate school behavior is maintained by "normal" accepted reinforcers.

In summary, some sort of reinforcer maintains our behavior from childhood through adulthood. The nature of that reinforcer may change from external to internal, but it still exists. While behavior change programs are initially external and artificial by nature, they do not have to remain so and if they do, they were not effectively designed. We believe that being altruistic and self-actualized is not arrived at through some mysterious and unexplainable process, but rather is the result of intrinsic reinforcement. As caretakers, we can help our children achieve their potential through providing a home environment which consistently makes positive reinforcement contingent on behaviors which will prepare the child to live a happy and successful life.

References

Amsworth, M. D., Bell, S. M. V. and Stayton, D. J. Individual differences in stranger situation behavior of one year olds. In H. R. Schaffer (Ed.) *The Origins Of Human Social Relations*. New York: Academic Press, 1971.

Azrin, N. H. & Foxx, R. M. *Toilet Training In Less Than A Day*. New York: Simon and Schuster, 1974.

Azrin, N. H. & Holtz, W. C. Punishment. In W. K. Honig (Ed.), *Operant Behavior: Areas of Research and Application*. New York: Appleton-Century-Crofts, 380–447, 1966.

Baumrind, D. Child care practices anteceding three patterns of preschool behavior. *Genetic Psychology Monographs*, 1967, *75*, 43–88.

Baumrind, D. Current patterns of parental authority. *Developmental Psychology Monographs*, 1971, No. 1, 1–103.

Becker, W. C. *Parents Are Teachers*. Champaign, Ill.: Research Press, 1971.

Bruner, J. S., Olver, R. R. & Greenfield, P. M. (eds.) *Studies in Cognitive Growth*. New York: Wiley, 1966.

Dreikus, R. *Children: The Challenge*. New York: Hawthorn Books, 1964.

Erikson, E. H. *Childhood and Society*. (2nd ed.) New York: Norton, 1963.

Faber, A. & Mazlish, E. *Liberated Parents Liberated Children*. New York: Avon Books, 1974.

Ginott, H. G. *Between Parent and Child*. New York: Avon Books, 1965.

Glasser, W. *Schools Without Failure*. New York: Perennial Library, 1969.

Gordon, T. *Parent Effectiveness Training*. New York: A Plume Book, 1975.

Haley, J. *Strategies of Psychotherapy*. New York: Grune & Stratton, 1963.

Halverson, H. M. An experimental study of prehension in infants by means of systematic cinema records. *Genetic Psychology Monographs.*, 1931, *10*, 107–286.

Hartig, M. & Kanfer, F. H. The role of verbal self-instructions in children's resistance to temptation. *Journal of Personality and Social Psychology*, 1973.

Irwin, O. C. Speech development in the young child. *Journal of Speech and Hearing Disorders*, 1952, *17*, 269–279.

Kubler-Ross, E. *On Death and Dying*. New York: Macmillan, 1969.

Kurtines, W. & Grief, E. B. The development of moral thought: Review and evaluation of Kohlberg's approach. *Psychological Bulletin*, 1974, *81*, 453–470, *125*, 259–267.

Leboyer, F. *Birth Without Violence.* New York: Knopf, 1975.

Malott, R. W. Contingency management in education. Kalamazoo: Behaviordelia, 1972.

Meyers, E. S., Ball, H. H., & Crutchfield, M. *The Kindergarten Teacher's Handbook.* Los Angeles: Gramery Press, 1973.

Mischel, W. & Ebbesen, E. Attention in delay of gratification. *Journal of Personality and Social Psychology,* 1970, *16,* 329–337.

Nelson, N. M. *et. al.* A randomized clinical trail of the Leboyer approach to childbirth. *New England Journal of Medicine,* 1980, *302,* 655–660.

Pavlov, I. P. *Conditioned Reflexes.* Translated by G. V. Anrep. London: Oxford, 1927. Originally published in Russian.

Perkins, D. G. and Perkins, F. M. *Nailbiting and Cuticlebiting: Kicking the Habit.* Richardson, Tx.: Self Control Press, 1976.

Piaget, J. *The Developmental Psychology of Jean Piaget.* New York: Van Nostrand, 1963.

Rheingold, H. L. The modification of social responsiveness in institutional babies. *Monographs of the Society for Research in Child Development.* 1956, *2*(2, Serial No. 63).

Satir, V. *Conjoint Family Therapy.* Palo Alto: Science and Behavior Books, 1964.

Satir, V. *Peoplemaking.* Palo Alto: Science and Behavior Books, 1972.

Schaffer, H. R. & Emerson, P. E. The development of social attachments in infancy. *Monographs of the Society of Research in Child Development,* 1964, *29*(3, Serial No. 94).

Seligman, M. E. P. *Helplessness: On Depression, Development, and Death.* San Francisco: Freeman, 1975.

Shirley, M. M. The first two years. University of Minnesota Press. *Institute of Child Welfare Monograph* No. 7, 1961.

Skinner, B. F. *Science and Human Behavior.* New York: Macmillan Co., 1953.

Smith, M. E. An investigation of the development of the sentence and the extent of vocabulary in young children. University of Iowa Study Child Welfare, 1926, *3* No. 5.

Trotter, R. J. Leboyer's babies. *Science News.* Jan. 22, 1977, 59.

DATE DUE